WHAT EVERY INVESTOR NEEDS TO KNOW ABOUT ACCOUNTING FRAUD

WHAT EVERY INVESTOR NEEDS TO KNOW ABOUT ACCOUNTING FRAUD

Jeff Madura

McGraw-Hill

New York   Chicago   San Francisco   Lisbon
London   Madrid   Mexico City   Milan   New Delhi
San Juan   Seoul   Singapore   Sydney   Toronto

HF
5686
.C7
M317
2004

The McGraw·Hill Companies

Library of Congress Cataloging-in-Publication Data

Madura, Jeff.
    What you need to know about accounting fraud / by Jeff Madura.— 1st
    ed.
    p.   cm.
    ISBN 0-07-142276-5 (pbk. : alk. paper)
    1. Corporations—Accounting—Corrupt practices—United States. 2.
    Corporations—Accounting—Corrupt practices—United States—Prevention.
    I. Title.

    HF5686.C7M317 2004
    332.63'2042—dc21   2003006581

1 2 3 4 5 6 7 8 9 0   DOC/DOC   0 9 8 7 6 5 4 3

ISBN 0-07-142276-5

McGraw-Hill books are available at special quantity discounts to use as premiums
and sales promotions, or for use in corporate training programs. For more information, please write to the Director of Special Sales, McGraw-Hill Professional, Two
Penn Plaza, New York, NY 10121-2298. Or contact your local bookstore.

This book is printed on recycled, acid-free paper containing a
minimum of 50% recycled, de-inked fiber.

Contents

WHAT EVERY INVESTOR NEEDS TO KNOW ABOUT ACCOUNTING FRAUD

CHAPTER

1

THE

ACCOUNTING

MESS

THE FINANCIAL SCANDALS involving firms such as Enron, World-Com, and Global Crossing have provided several lessons for investors:

1. A firm's executives do not necessarily make decisions that are in the best interests of the investors who own the firm's stock.
2. A firm's board of directors does not necessarily ensure that the firm's managers serve shareholders' interests.
3. A firm's financial statements do not necessarily reflect its financial condition.
4. Independent auditors do not necessarily ensure that a firm's financial statements are valid.

INVESTOR CYNICISM

These financial scandals have created a new cynicism in the financial community. The most basic ground rules of corporate responsibility to investors have been violated.

If investors cannot rely on executives, board members, or auditors for valid information about a firm, investing in a stock is essentially a form of uninformed gambling. However, there is a difference between gambling with a small amount of funds as a source of entertainment and investing for retirement or other future needs. There are many true stories of investors who struck it rich by investing in a stock that was unknown at the time. However, there are many more cases in which investors lost most or all of their investment as a result of buying stocks on the basis of inaccurate information.

One of the most common reasons why investors incur large losses is that they have too much faith in the information provided to them by neighbors, friends, brokers, analysts, and the firm's executives. Unethical behavior on the part of some executives is not a new phenomenon. However, investors are less likely to detect or complain about such behavior when stock market conditions are as favorable as they were in the late 1990s. Had investors been more cynical in the late 1990s, they would not have had as much confidence in some stocks as they did. Consequently, they would not have driven stock prices up so high.

In the past, even when investors incurred losses on investments, they tolerated unethical behavior. Many investors prefer to keep their investment losses confidential. Others realize that their losses may be attributed to their own poor decision making and not to unethical behavior on the part of accountants or financial market participants. Moreover, unethical behavior by a firm's accountants, executives, directors, or independent auditors may be difficult to prove.

The events in the 2001–2002 period are reminiscent of those of the late 1980s, when the market for high-risk (junk) bonds fell apart. At that time, junk bonds were highly valued because investors relied too heavily on the brokers who sold junk bonds for advice and recommendations. Investors learned about the risk of junk bonds when economic conditions deteriorated and some issuers of these bonds began to default on their obligations. In a similar manner, investors were taken by surprise by the accounting scandals of 2001–2002, and securities were revalued once investors were better informed about the firms that issued securities. However, one major difference between the financial scandals of 2001–2002 and the junk bond crash is that more investors were exposed to the stock market in 2001–2002 than had been exposed to junk bonds. Consequently, more investors took a hit in the 2001–2002 period than during the junk bond crash in the late 1980s.

The savings and loan crisis also occurred in the late 1980s. Many savings institutions that investors perceived to be safe took excessive risks (including investments in junk bonds) and ultimately failed. In the 1990s, the media referred to the 1980s as the decade of greed because of the junk bond crisis and the savings institution crisis. Yet new scandals emerged in the 1990s. The treasurer of Orange County, California, used county funds to make inappropriate risky investments and caused massive losses for the county. Long-Term Capital Management (a mutual fund of a special type) experienced major losses on its investments as a result of poor portfolio management, and was bailed out by the government. Consequently, it can be argued that the 1990s differed from the 1980s only in the form of greed that was applied in the financial markets.

In the early 2000s, the major scandals were related to financial reporting, ratings assigned by analysts, and insider trading. The unethical behavior of the late 1980s was not eliminated in the 1990s or in the early twenty-first century, it simply took on a new form.

The regulators of the accounting industry and the financial markets were publicly embarrassed by the financial scandals. They took initiatives to regain their credibility. The regulators imposed rules that were intended to make executives accountable for their actions. Independent accounting firms were put on notice to properly do the auditing for which they are compensated. Directors, who oversee a firm's operations, were put on notice to perform the monitoring tasks for which they are compensated.

Even with all the publicity about corporate government reforms that are supposed to prevent faulty accounting, consider the following events that occurred in 2003:

- The Securities and Exchange Commission (SEC) reviewed drafts of annual reports of all Fortune 500 firms. It sent written comments of concerns to 350 of these firms. In particular, it had concerns about the limited financial data provided in the drafts, a lack of clarity (transparency), and methods of estimating numbers. Specifically, some firms are not fully disclosing the material year-to-year changes and other information that indicates their cash flow situation. They are not explaining the accounting policies properly or the assumptions they used within the accounting function. They are not explaining how they derived the numbers for key items such as intangible assets.

- AOL and the Securities and Exchange Commission were arguing about the degree to which AOL overstated its revenue. AOL estimated that it overstated revenue by $190 million, but the SEC believed that the overstatement should be higher.

- The federal mortgage agency called Freddie Mac was investigated due to faulty accounting.

- Bristol-Myers announced that it would need to restate its earnings because of numerous accounting violations that overstated earnings.

- Tyco acknowledged some accounting errors that required an accounting adjustment of more than $1 billion for the second quarter of 2003. This occurred after Tyco hired accountants and attorneys to clean up its books following its accounting scandal in 2002. That effort, which led to 55,000 hours of audit work and cost Tyco $55 million, apparently was not sufficient to detect the faulty accounting.

- Beyond the more blatant accounting errors, investors are still subjected to a general lack of transparency. Important financial information about expenses and revenue is still commonly buried in a footnote. Many annual reports continue to serve as a public relations campaign rather than full disclosure of the firm's financial condition.

EVOLUTION OF ZERO-TOLERANCE INVESTING

The publicity about unethical behavior in financial markets is giving birth to a new attitude of zero tolerance. Investors realize that even with more stringent rules, there will still be criminal activity in financial markets that could destroy the value of their investments. They need to take matters into their own hands by adopting a zero-tolerance attitude. Some investors may take the extreme approach of completely avoiding all investments in stocks or other securities. However, this strategy forgoes valuable opportunities. Stocks generally outperform bank deposits or Treasury securities over the long run. Therefore, a compromise for investors is to consider only investments (including stocks) in which the risk of fraudulent reporting or other related unethical behavior is minimal. This book suggests how the zero-tolerance attitude can be used to capitalize on investing in the stock market in the long run, while reducing exposure to deceptive reporting practices and other unethical behavior in financial markets.

There are four rules of zero-tolerance investing:

1. *Be suspicious of the firms in which you are considering an investment.* Some firms have unethical executives who mislead investors with deceptive accounting or spend cash in ways that benefit themselves instead of the firm's shareholders. Other firms have incompetent executives or managers, resulting in bad managerial decisions even if the intentions were appropriate. Your investment in any stock could be subject to a major loss as a result of unethical or incompetent management.

2. *Recognize your limitations.* You cannot necessarily detect firms that use deceptive accounting or that waste cash because of the unethical or incompetent behavior of their managers.

3. *Recognize the limitations of investment advisers.* Like some corporate executives, some investment advisers are either unethical or incompetent. Furthermore, even the most competent and ethical advisers are not necessarily able to detect a firm's unethical reporting practices. There are numerous cases of well-known stocks that have experienced a pronounced decline in price without any advance warning from investment advisers.

4. *Diversify your investments.* You need to diversify so that you are not excessively exposed to any single investment whose value may ultimately be affected by misleading accounting or other unethical behavior on the part of the firm's executives.

This book reinforces these four rules of zero-tolerance investing. Part I explains the different ways in which misleading accounting practices can distort stock valuations. Part II explains why accounting controls cannot be trusted. Part III explains how boards of directors can prevent deceptive accounting. Part IV suggests how governance may prevent deceptive accounting. Part V describes how investors can cope with deceptive accounting.

I

How Accounting Can Distort Stock Valuations

C H A P T E R

2

THE LINK
BETWEEN
ACCOUNTING
AND STOCK
VALUATION

DECISIONS CONCERNING stock investments are based on valuations. Investors purchase stocks when their valuation is higher than the prevailing stock price, and they sell some of their holdings when their valuation is lower than the prevailing stock price. Investors who conduct valuations and correctly determine when a stock is improperly priced can earn high returns on their investments.

THE INFLUENCE OF ACCOUNTING ON VALUATION

Investors who use financial statements in valuing a firm's stock rely on the accuracy of the numbers reported by the firm's accountants and audited by an independent auditor. The two financial statements that are commonly used in the valuation process are the income statement and the balance sheet.

Income Statement

A firm's income statement reports the firm's revenue and expenses over a particular period. Earnings represent the difference between a firm's revenue and its expenses.

Balance Sheet

The balance sheet indicates a firm has obtained funds, and how it has used them as of a particular point in time. A balance sheet has two components: (1) assets and (2) liabilities and shareholders' equity. A firm's assets represent how it has invested its funds. Assets are classified as short-term assets (such as inventory or accounts receivable), which normally have a life of 1 year or less, and long-term assets (such as machinery or buildings), which have a long life. Liabilities represent what the firm owes. Short-term liabilities are accounts payable and other borrowed funds that will be paid off within the year. Long-term liabilities represent debt with maturities beyond 1 year. Shareholders' equity represents the investment in the firm by its owners.

The two components of the balance sheet should be equal, so that the assets are equal to liabilities plus shareholders' equity. In other words, when the firm obtains funds by borrowing or by allowing investors to purchase its equity, it uses those funds to invest in assets. The composition of liabilities and shareholders' equity indicates the amount of risk taken by the firm. In general, firms with a higher level of debt are more likely to experience debt repayment problems. However, other factors also need to be considered, such as whether the firm generates sufficient revenue to cover its interest payments and other expenses.

Proxy Statement

Investors should also review the proxy statement, which provides information about some business relationships in a section that is often called "related party transactions." This section should disclose relationships that could trigger concern, such as whether the board members work for firms that receive substantial income from the firm of which they are directors. Not all relationships listed in this section are cause for alarm.

As of 2001, the Securities and Exchange Commission (SEC) requires that the proxy statement disclose information about accounting fees, such as the amount of nonauditing (consulting) fees that were paid by the firm to its auditors.

Cash Flow and Earnings Information

You can review the firm's 10-Q or 10-K filings to compare the change in earnings to the change in cash flow. The cash flow information is disclosed as "cash from operations" or "cash from operating activities." Cash flows are not as easy to manipulate as earnings. If there is a large increase in earnings without any improvement in cash flow, investors must question whether the company is receiving any benefit from the higher level of reported earnings. Some investors lose sight of the fact that the reason for focusing on earnings is to derive future cash flows. If the change in earnings does not serve as an indicator of future cash flows, then the expected future cash flows should not be adjusted in response to an increase in earnings.

In April 2001, Enron reported quarterly earnings of $425 million. In May 2001, it filed its 10-Q statement with the SEC, showing that its cash flow had been reduced by $464 million in the same quarter. Looking back, this discrepancy should have triggered suspicion among investors. The term *quality of earnings* is now commonly used to reflect the degree to which the reported earnings truly reflect earnings. When the earnings numbers are not backed by cash flow numbers, the quality of earnings may be poor.

VALUATION METHODS

Two of the most common methods for valuing stocks are described here. Regardless of the valuation method used, faulty accounting can complicate the valuation process.

Cash Flow Method

While investors have different opinions as to how a stock should be valued, all investors agree that the expected future cash flows are relevant. Some investors attempt to forecast a firm's future cash flows and then determine the present value of those future cash flows. If, for example, this method results in an estimate of $300 million, and if there are 10 million shares out-standing, the value per share is

$$\text{Value per share} = \$300,000,000/10,000,000$$
$$= \$30$$

The limitation with this approach is that future cash flows are difficult to predict. Firms do not normally provide forecasts of cash flows, so investors tend to use the earnings information in recent financial state-ments to derive cash flow forecasts.

If all of a firm's revenue is received in cash and all of its expenses are paid in cash, then the earnings will be a good measure of cash flow. In real-ity, however, most firms have some noncash expenses, such as deprecia-tion. For example, if a firm purchases a building or machinery, it amortizes (spreads) the expense over several years. If the expense is $10 million, it may apply a depreciation expense of $1 million per year for 10 years (the exact amount of depreciation applied each year would be based on the depreciation rules at the time the accounting is performed). Investors can attempt to separate the actual cash expenses from the noncash expenses. You can also count only the revenue that represents a cash payment. By focusing on cash transactions, you derive an estimate of cash flows. Then you must apply your expected growth rate to the cash flows over time. Next, you determine the present value of the future cash flows. That is, you discount the future cash flows using a discount rate that reflects the return that is required by investors who invest in that firm's stock. The discount rate is commonly within a range of 10 to 25 percent. A higher discount rate is used for firms with riskier cash flows, which essentially reduces the val-uation of firms that have more risk.

Limitations of the Cash Flow Method   One problem with the cash flow method is that cash flows in a particular period will not necessarily indi-cate future cash flows. For example, a sudden increase in cash flows can occur when a firm reduces its spending on research and development or on machinery. However, if the reduction in these forms of investment today will force the firm to increase its investment in the future, then the firm's cash outflows will increase in the future and its net cash flows will decrease.

Information about a firm's cash flow is limited. Investors commonly attempt to derive an estimate of a firm's cash flows from its reported earn-ings. However, since the earnings are often exaggerated, investors are likely to overestimate a firm's cash flows.

Another limitation of the cash flow method is the difficulty of estimating the growth rate of cash flows. If the growth rate that is applied to the forecasted cash flows is inaccurate, your valuation will be inaccurate. In addition, the discount rate that you apply to future cash flows is subjective. If you apply a discount rate that is too low, you will overestimate the valuation. ·

Price/Earnings Method

An alternative valuation approach is to apply a price/earnings (P/E) multiple to the firm's earnings per share. Each publicly traded firm has a price/earnings ratio, measured as its stock price per share divided by its earnings per share. For example, if the firm is expected to earn $2 per share next year and the average price/earnings ratio of other similar publicly traded firms in the industry is 10, its valuation could be derived as

$$10 \times \$2 \text{ per share} = \$20 \text{ per share}$$

The price/earnings ratios for various firms in an industry are provided by many online investment web sites. The expected earnings are normally derived from an assessment of recent earnings. Even if earnings are expected to change, the recent earnings are used as the basis for deriving a forecast of the future earnings.

Limitations of the Price/Earnings Method   The P/E method also has limitations. Some firms in an industry may have better growth prospects than other firms in that same industry, yet, when you apply the mean industry price/earnings ratio to a firm, you are implicitly assuming that the potential growth rate of the firm you are assessing is the same as that of the industry.

Also, the P/E method is not applicable to a firm that has negative earnings. To avoid that limitation, some investors use a price/revenue multiple instead of the price/earnings ratio. They estimate the firm's revenue per share and multiply it by the price/revenue multiple of the industry in order to derive a value for the firm's stock.

Some investors rely on a firm's past earnings or revenue performance in making investment decisions. However, past performance is not necessarily an accurate indicator of the future, and the prevailing price of the firm's stock should already reflect expectations concerning the future. That is, high-performing firms are already valued high to reflect investor expectations. If a firm had strong earnings recently, but its stock is priced at 50 times its annual earnings per share, it may be overvalued.

The valuation derived using the P/E method is subject to the accounting used to determine earnings. A firm that inflates its reported earnings for the present year may be able to inflate the value of its stock, at least temporarily. Alternatively, a firm that uses less creative accounting methods may report lower earnings than its competitors just because of its conservative reporting. Consequently, its value may be underestimated if investors apply the industry P/E to its reported earnings.

A firm may also be able to manipulate its stock price by disguising its industry. If it performs operations that fit into various industries, it would prefer to be classified in the industry in which the price/earnings multiples of other firms are high. In this way, it will be assigned a higher value for a given level of earnings. Enron not only distorted its earnings, but even distorted the industry in which it operated. One of its main businesses was trading various types of energy derivative contracts. Yet, it did not want to be known as a trading company because the price/earnings multiples of companies that engage in trading are relatively low.

IMPACT OF THE FIRM'S RISK ON VALUE

Another characteristic that investors should consider when valuing a firm's stock is its risk, which reflects the uncertainty surrounding the return from investing in the stock. The ultimate adverse effect of this uncertainty is that the firm goes bankrupt, causing investors to lose 100 percent of their investment.

Given two firms of a similar size, with similar historical earnings, and in the same industry, the firm with the lower level of risk should have a higher value. Since investors tend to prefer less risk, they assign a higher valuation to a stock that has less risk, other factors (such as expected return) being held equal.

Measuring Risk

When firms invest in assets, their funding comes from either equity (investment by stockholders) or debt (funds provided by creditors). For a given level of earnings, the return on shareholders' investment (equity) is higher when the assets are supported with more debt. To illustrate, consider two firms that each have $100 million in assets. Firm A's assets are supported with $50 million of equity and $50 million of debt. Firm B's assets are supported with $60 million of equity and $40 million of debt. Assume that both firms had earnings after taxes of $8 million. The return on assets (ROA) for each firm is

$$ROA = \text{earnings after taxes/total assets}$$
$$= \$8,000,000/\$100,000,000$$
$$= 8\%$$

However, investors tend to focus on the return on their equity (ROE), which is measured as

$$ROE = \text{earnings after taxes/equity invested in the firm}$$

For Firms A and B, the ROE is

$$\text{ROE for Firm A} = \$8,000,000/\$50,000,000$$
$$= 16\%$$
$$\text{ROE for Firm B} = \$8,000,000/\$60,000,000$$
$$= 13.3\%$$

While the two firms have the same ROA, Firm A has a higher ROE because it uses a smaller level of equity to support its assets. However, the downside of using a small amount of equity is that a larger amount of debt is needed to support the assets. The larger the amount of debt used, the larger the periodic interest payments that must be made will be. These debt payments can squeeze a firm's cash flows and increase the risk that the firm will go bankrupt. A higher risk of a firm's going bankrupt translates into a higher level of risk for investors in that firm.

Given the impact of the debt level, investors monitor a firm's risk by assessing the firm's balance sheet. One popular measure of risk is the debt ratio, measured as

$$\text{Debt/total assets}$$

The debt ratios for the two firms are

$$\text{Debt ratio for Firm A} = \$50,000,000/\$100,000,000$$
$$= 50\%$$
$$\text{Debt ratio for Firm B} = \$40,000,000/\$100,000,000$$
$$= 40\%$$

Based on the information provided, Firm A has more risk than Firm B.

Limitations of Measuring Risk

A measurement of risk based on a balance sheet alone is subject to error. The firm's cash flows over time should also be assessed, because firms with more stable cash flows are more capable of meeting their debt payments. That is, a firm with a relatively high debt load may be capable of handling that load if it also has sufficient cash flow to cover the interest payments. Conversely, a firm with a lower debt level may be more risky if it experiences very volatile cash flows in some periods. When its cash inflows are very low, it may not be able to cover even a small amount of interest payments on its debt.

3

BACKGROUND ON DECEPTIVE ACCOUNTING

THE NEXT SEVERAL chapters explain how accounting methods can distort the financial measures that investors use to value stocks. When the financial measures are distorted, the valuations of stocks may be distorted as well. Investors who recognize these distortions can attempt to limit their exposure to stocks that may be subjected to accounting manipulation.

BACKGROUND ON ACCOUNTING GUIDELINES

The general guidelines on how to measure a firm's earnings, expenses, and other financial statement items are referred to as generally accepted accounting principles (GAAP). The Financial Accounting Standards Board sets these guidelines. The guidelines allow some flexibility in the accounting in specific circumstances. Unfortunately, some firms take advantage of this flexibility by using whatever accounting method within the guidelines that generates the most favorable numbers. Firms recognize that their stock may be given a higher value if they show higher earnings or cash flows.

HOW THE GUIDELINES ENCOURAGE DECEPTIVE ACCOUNTING

Recall that the most common valuation methods involve the estimation of a firm's future cash flows and the application of a price/earnings multiple to the firm's earnings. To the extent that a firm's accounting can affect the firm's reported earnings, it can also affect investors' valuation of that firm. Thus, investors should be cautious when they interpret earnings or other numbers provided in a firm's financial statements. Regardless of the exact valuation method used, recent reported earnings will have a major influence on the valuation. A higher level of earnings is likely to lead to higher cash flow estimates when a firm is valued on the present value of expected future cash flows. It will also lead to a higher valuation when the price/earnings multiple is applied to a recent earnings level.

If executives can develop strategies that will increase revenue by more than they increase expenses, or that will reduce expenses by a larger amount than they reduce revenue, they will generally be able to increase earnings. Some executives use effective business strategies to achieve this goal. Others may simply attempt to manipulate the level of reported earnings by using deceptive accounting methods. Some of these methods inflate revenue without inflating expenses. Others do not account for expenses in the period in which the expenses occurred. To the extent that executives can use accounting methods to manipulate the report of recent earnings, they can manipulate the valuation of the firm's stock, at least in the short run.

Given the substantial flexibility in accounting methods, two firms with the exact same level of sales and expenses may report distinctly different earnings. Consequently, firms can easily make their earnings look better in a particular reporting period while remaining within the accounting guidelines. Such manipulation may cause future earnings to be lower, but executives who are planning to sell large holdings of the firm's stock may prefer to inflate earnings now. While this form of earnings manipulation is unethical, it is not necessarily illegal. Therefore, investors cannot presume that accounting firms or the Securities and Exchange Commission (SEC) will prevent this type of abuse from occurring.

Even if the accounting rules are changed, there will always be some degree of arbitrary judgment in the reporting of revenue, expenses, and earnings. Since there will always be opportunities to inflate earnings within a particular period, a firm's earnings may not always represent its financial condition. In fact, a firm that falls short of its earnings forecast may be motivated to manipulate the reported earnings in order to meet the forecast.

Enron consistently achieved its reported earnings forecast, which helped to create a false perception of its stable performance.

SMOOTHING EARNINGS

While the Enron case was an extreme example of deceptive accounting, many firms use accounting methods that complicate the interpretation of their financial statements. Since many investors and analysts derive expected cash flows from earnings, they frequently reward firms that have stable earnings. Consider the earnings per share (total earnings divided by number of shares) of the following two firms over the last eight quarters:

Quarter	Firm A	Firm B
1	$2.00	$2.00
2	4.00	2.20
3	1.00	1.80
4	3.00	1.90
5	−1.00	2.10
6	4.00	2.05
7	2.00	1.95
8	1.00	2.00

Both firms have a mean earnings per share of $2.00. However, Firm B would probably be rated higher, assuming that other characteristics of the firms are similar. Investors who review past earnings would expect Firm B's future performance to be more predictable. They would be less concerned about the possibility that Firm B would have very weak performance in the future, and they are willing to pay a higher price for stocks that exhibit less risk.

Now suppose you are an accountant for Firm A. You have two choices:

1. Use accounting methods that accurately reflect your situation.
2. Use accounting methods that are within the accounting guidelines and that smooth reported earnings over time.

If you believe that investors prefer income to be stable from one year to the next, which alternative would you prefer for reporting purposes? It would be rational for you to smooth earnings. However, some creative accounting tactics go beyond smoothing income and are clearly a misrepresentation of the firm's business transactions or financial condition.

IMPACT OF THE RETIREMENT PLAN ON EARNINGS

A firm's reported earnings can be influenced by its retirement plan. Consider a firm that has a defined benefit plan for its employees. When its retirement fund performs well because of strong market conditions, it will generate a higher return than is needed to cover future retirement benefits. Thus, the retirement plan can generate earnings for the firm. However, earnings derived in this manner are not the result of normal operations, and it would be a mistake to presume that these earnings will be consistently generated in the future. Investors should separate this income from operating income if they are using recent income to project future cash flows.

When firms provide defined retirement benefits for their employees, they must set aside an amount that will be sufficient to pay those retirement benefits in the future. These funds are invested by the firm, and their future value is difficult to predict. If firms believe that they do not have sufficient funds to cover the future retirement benefits, they must add to the pension fund, and this is recorded as an expense in the quarter in which it occurs.

However, firms have some flexibility in deciding whether they must add to their pension fund. They estimate how much the value of their pension fund will grow and therefore what the value will be in the future using an assumed rate of return on the pension fund. For example, a firm may assume that its pension fund investments will generate a return of 10 percent a year. The higher the assumed rate of return, the smaller the amount of money that must be set aside to cover future retirement benefits. Thus, a firm can reduce the amount of funds that it needs to hold in its pension fund by increasing the assumed rate of return on the fund's investments. After increasing the assumed rate of return on the pension fund, a firm might even determine that the pension plan is overfunded. That is, with the higher return, it can achieve the amount it will need with fewer funds. This adjustment can boost reported earnings.

The danger of this adjustment is that if the assumed return is excessive, it will ultimately cause the firm's pension fund to be underfunded. When this happens, the firm will have to add more money to the pension fund, which is an expense. Furthermore, investors must be careful to recognize when an increase in earnings is a result of an adjustment in the pension fund rather than coming from operations. An adjustment in the pension fund does not reflect an improvement in the firm's sales or a reduction in the firm's expenses. Yet, some investors may mistakenly believe the firm's operations have improved when they notice an increase in earnings that is due to a pension fund adjustment.

By the end of 2002, Caterpillar's retirement plan was underfunded by about $2.8 billion, while General Motors's retirement plan was underfunded by more than $20 billion. The defined benefit pension funds for the 500 firms in the Standard & Poor's 500 index were underfunded by about $240 billion. Some firms build up their pension fund with their own stock. Yet this requires placing more of their own stock in the market (in which their pension funds are investors), which can reduce the value of the shares.

4

HOW ACCOUNTING CAN BE USED TO INFLATE REVENUE

WHEN INVESTORS use a method based on revenue to value a firm, the valuation will be excessive if the revenue is exaggerated. If investors derive cash flow estimates from reported revenue, exaggerated revenue will result in an overestimate of cash flows and thus an overestimate of value. Alternatively, if investors use a price/revenue ratio, the reported revenue will influence value. If the industry norm is a price/revenue ratio of 2 and the firm reports revenue of $15 per share, the estimated value of the firm will be $30 per share when the price/revenue ratio is applied. However, the firm would have reported revenue of $13 per share if it had used a more traditional method of measuring revenue, its estimated value would have been $26 per share when the price/revenue ratio was applied. Even if investors use a price/earnings ratio, inflated revenue will still affect the stock valuation because it will result in inflated earnings. Thus, the industry price/earnings ratio will be applied to an overestimated earnings level.

Many firms have inflated their earnings by inflating their revenue. In 2002, the Securities and Exchange Commission (SEC) initiated an investigation of firms that used questionable methods for estimating their revenue. The firms investigated included CMS Energy Corp., Dynergy, Reliant Resources Inc., Global Crossing Ltd., Lucent Technologies, and Quest Communications. Some of the methods that have been used to inflate revenue are identified here.

REPORTING FUTURE REVENUE

Some service firms that receive multiyear contracts from clients record all the revenue in the first year of the contract, even when they have received payment only for the first year. Some Internet firms that generate revenue from online membership subscriptions count potential renewals when they record their sales for the year. Some firms report all of their sales as revenue even when the cash has not been received. When a large portion of the sales are credit sales, the cash flow attributed to those sales will either occur in a future period or not occur at all.

In April 2002, Gemstar (owner of TV Guide) used a method for reporting revenue that includes orders not yet paid by customers. This accounting method is not illegal, but investors recognized that the reported revenue might have overestimated cash inflows because some of the cash had not yet been collected. Once analysts recognized that this accounting method was used, the company's stock price quickly declined by more than 30 percent.

REPORTING CANCELED ORDERS AS REVENUE

Sunbeam used a selling strategy that made it easy for customers to cancel orders. Yet it counted all the orders it received as revenue, even though it was likely that many of them would be canceled. In 1998, Sunbeam restated earnings for the six previous quarters. One of the reasons was that it had overstated its revenue, which resulted in overstated earnings.

In 2001, when the SEC filed a complaint against Xerox concerning the company's financial reporting, one of the main issues was that Xerox had included expected future revenue from suppliers within its reported revenue. In April 2002, Xerox paid a $10 million fine to the SEC as a result of the manner in which it had estimated its revenue from leasing its copiers and printers. Xerox also agreed to restate earnings over a 4-year period.

Given the wide flexibility that firms have when reporting revenue and earnings, they have to stretch the rules a long way before they are forced to restate earnings. However, while a restatement is appropriate as a means of correcting the error, it does not correct the losses suffered by investors who purchased the stock based on their analysis of the firm's financial statements. It also does not correct the gains that executives may have realized from selling their holdings of the firm's shares over the period during which the earnings were inflated.

REPORTING PRODUCTS ALLOCATED TO DISTRIBUTORS AS REVENUE

Some manufacturing firms book revenue when they allocate their products to their distributors. However, the distributors are not the ultimate purchasers of the product, as they must attempt to sell the products for the firms. If the distributors do not sell the products, they will return them to the manufacturers. Therefore, the revenue will be overstated. Even if the products allocated to the distributor are sold in the next year, this accounting method inflates the reported sales and therefore the reported earnings for the present year.

Consider how a firm that serves as an intermediary might report revenue. Assume that you have a business that serves as an intermediary between a steel firm and various car manufacturers. Assume that over the last year, the supplier has paid you $100,000 for helping it to sell steel valued at $3 million. What is your revenue for the year? The logical response is $100,000, since that is the amount of funds that you received in return for providing your service. However, using creative accounting, you might claim revenue of $3 million for the year by arguing that the steel was yours momentarily before it was purchased by the car manufacturers.

Priceline.com has used this accounting method, which explains how it could achieve a revenue of more than $1 billion per year. That is, Priceline's accounting suggests that Priceline owns the products that it sells for others.

REPORTING SECURITY TRADES AS REVENUE

Some firms trade various types of derivative securities whose values are tied to commodities or other securities. These firms hope to buy the contracts for less than they sell them for. A traditional method of accounting for such a contract is to report the "net," or the difference between the amount received from selling the contract and the amount paid for the contract. This net is reported in a section of the income statement called "trading gains and losses." For example, if a firm purchases a contract for $260,000 and sells that contract for $300,000, it would report a $40,000 net from the contract. An alternative method of accounting is to report the "gross," with the $300,000 received from selling the contract being classified as revenue. Critics contend that such a method is misleading because it allows a firm to generate revenue simply by purchasing contracts and selling them. Firms can create the appearance of revenue growth simply by trading more contracts every year. Even if they sell the contracts for the same price at which they purchased them, they can report the sale of the contracts as revenue. Enron used this type of accounting when it traded various types of energy contracts. This accounting method magnified the size of Enron's operations and was a major reason for Enron's reported revenue growth during the late 1990s.

Many other energy firms also used this type of accounting method, so Enron might have argued that it was the convention within the industry. Two firms could have the exact same operations, but the firm that reports gross will appear to have more revenue than the firm that reports net. If analysts and other investors have the ability to recognize the difference between net and gross reporting, perhaps the accounting method used does not matter. However, the fact that many firms in the energy industry use the accounting method that inflates revenue seems to suggest that they are better off with that method. That is, by following the "industry standard," each firm can keep up with its competitors by providing equally misleading reports of revenue. It should not be surprising that firms use whatever means they can within the guidelines to present their financial position in the most optimistic perspective.

In April 2002, it was made public that Dynergy had used optimistic valuations of its contracts to buy or sell natural gas. Such valuations are not illegal, as accounting guidelines allow much flexibility. However, this form of accounting can be misleading to investors.

Investors can review the footnotes of financial statements to catch a creative accounting method that exaggerates a firm's revenue. However, many investors will not have the resources to detect the accounting methods used by some firms. The analysis of financial statements could be done much more efficiently if investors did not have to waste their time trying to correct for inflated revenue numbers reported by some firms.

5

HOW ACCOUNTING CAN DEFLATE EXPENSES

MANY FIRMS RECOGNIZE that investors and analysts focus on their operating efficiency and use accounting that will indicate reductions in operating expenses. The accounting methods used to achieve this goal are not necessarily illegal, but may be misleading to those investors and analysts who rely on financial statements. Many of the methods shift some operating expenses to other parts of the financial statements, so that operating expenses are reduced, and operating income (revenue minus operating expenses) is increased. Since some investors derive values of a firm according to its operating earnings, they may value a firm higher if it reduces its operating expenses as a means of increasing its operating earnings. Some of the common methods for deflating expenses are summarized next.

CLASSIFYING EXPENSES AS CAPITAL EXPENDITURES

A firm's common expenses such as labor and materials should be classified as operating expenses. Conversely, as mentioned in Chapter 3, the expense of a long-term asset such as machinery is depreciated over time because its use is spread over time. In the year that the asset is obtained, the reported expense is only a fraction of the total expense due to depreciation. Accountants are well aware of the difference between common operating expenses versus capital expenditures that allow for the expense to be spread over time.

WorldCom misclassified some of its operating expenses as capital expenditures. The result is that these expenses in 2000 and 2001 were underestimated, which caused its earnings to be overestimated. This faulty accounting was the primary reason why WorldCom's earnings were overstated by $3.85 billion over a five-quarter period.

CLASSIFYING EXPENSES AS WRITEOFFS

A writeoff is viewed as a one-time charge against earnings. For example, consider a firm with a subsidiary that was attempting to create a new product that would be added to the firm's product line. Assume that after a year, the firm gave up on the idea of adding a new product and it shut down the subsidiary. It could record the expense of this subsidiary as a writeoff.

The separation of a writeoff from other expenses is useful to investors because it indicates which expenses are nonrecurring.There is some flexibility within accounting guidelines on whether a particular expense is classified within a writeoff or under the firm's normal operating expenses. Using the previous example, labor costs incurred by the subsidiary may be part of the writeoff. What about general research and development expenses for the firm? Since these expenses would occur every year, they should not be included within the writeoff. Yet, the more expenses that the firm can include within the writeoff, the lower will be its normal operating expenses.

Assume that the direct costs of the subsidiary are $3,000,000. Yet, the firm has the accounting flexibility to include another $2,000,000 of general research and development expenses within the writeoff. The firm's income is shown in Exhibit 5.1.

EXHIBIT 5.1   How Accounting for Writeoffs Affects Valuation

	Accounting Method A	Accounting Method B
Revenue	$30,000,000	$30,000,000
Operating Expenses	24,000,000	22,000,000
Earnings Before Writeoff	6,000,000	8,000,000
Writeoff	3,000,000	5,000,000
Earnings After Writeoff	3,000,000	3,000,000
Earnings Per Share (before Writeoff)	$1.50	$2.00
Valuation of Stock (based on PE multiple of 20 times next year's future earnings, assuming no writeoff)	$30	$40

If investors interpret the writeoff to be a one-time expense, they may use the earnings level before the writeoff as a forecast of next year's earnings. Thus, investors would value the firm higher using Accounting Method B. To more directly illustrate how the accounting affects valuation, assume that the firm has 4 million shares of stock outstanding. If the firm uses Accounting Method A to report earnings, and if earnings before writeoffs is used by investors to predict next year's earnings, investors would forecast earnings to be $1.50 per share (computed as $6,000,000/4,000,000 shares). Alternatively, if the firm uses Accounting Method B to report earnings, investors would forecast earnings per share for next year to be $2 per share (computed as $8,000,000/4,000,000 shares). To determine how the different estimates lead to different valuations, assume that other firms in the same industry have a price-earnings (PE) multiple of 20. Notice the $10 difference in the valuation calculated with these two accounting methods.

This example is not exaggerated. During the 1996–2001 period, Allied Waste Industries averaged more than $200 million in annual after-tax profits. When considering the writeoffs, it averaged less than $50 million in annual after-tax profits. Compaq Computer's annual after-tax profits are reduced by more than 75 percent after considering writeoffs. International Paper's annual after-tax profits are reduced by more than 80 percent over the same period when considering writeoffs. In 1998, WorldCom attempted a writeoff of more than $7 billion following the acquisition of MCI; It reduced this estimate to about $3 billion after being questioned by the SEC.

Even if a firm does not hide any normal (year-to-year) expenses within a writeoff, investors should not presume that the writeoff is a one-time charge. Based on this presumption, investors would ignore the writeoff this year when attempting to predict expenses and earnings in future years. Some firms tend to have large and frequent writeoffs, although the writeoff in each period may be for a different reason. Investors who use earnings before writeoffs to predict future earnings will likely overestimate future earnings, and therefore overestimate the firm's value today.

Lack of Disclosure About Writeoffs

On October 16, 2001, Enron announced a $618 million loss. Yet, it did not disclose that it had a writeoff of $1.2 billion, which reduced its shareholders' equity by that amount. It is inconceivable that a financial announcement would fail to mention to the shareholders that their total equity investment had just been reduced by more than a billion dollars.

Writing Off Inventory Expenses

Rather than account for wasted inventory in the operating expenses, some firms commonly write off obsolete inventory. One common accounting tactic is to include inventory writeoffs with other writeoffs. An inventory writeoff represents a cost of holding some inventory that is no longer useful. For example, an inventory of products may be written off because the product has been discontinued. If the expense of wasted inventory was included within operating expenses, then it would be considered an expense that could occur in any period. However, when it is included in writeoffs, it might be perceived as a one-time cost that will not occur again. Therefore, when investors assess a firm's earnings to forecast future earnings or cash flows, they may ignore the writeoff. Yet, if firms consistently have inventory writeoffs, they are repeatedly incurring this expense. Investors who do not recognize the expense as recurring will underestimate the firm's future expenses, and will overestimate the firm's future earnings and cash flows. One indicator of a potential writedown of inventory is when inventory levels build up over time on quarterly financial statements, which could imply that there is some obsolete inventory that has not yet been eliminated and may be written off in the future.

CLASSIFYING EXPENSES AS NONRECURRING

When a firm forecasts its future earnings (called pro forma earnings), it excludes expenses that recently occurred but will not happen again. For example, a firm may incur expenses when it discontinues a product, because it will discard machinery and inventory. These expenses are considered to be "nonrecurring" because the product is no longer offered, and there should be no more expenses associated with the product. Therefore, it is logical to exclude those specific expenses when forecasting earnings.

However, some firms mistakenly ignore all nonrecurring expenses when forecasting earnings. If a firm discontinues a product every year, it will have a specific type of nonrecurring expense every year. In essence, the expense from discontinuing a product is a recurring expense, and should be considered when this firm forecasts earnings. For firms that have some form of restructuring charges every year, pro forma earnings that do not account for restructuring will likely be overestimated. Firms tend to be too optimistic when forecasting earnings, and one of the reasons is that firms are unwilling to recognize that some "nonrecurring" expenses will continue to occur.

CLASSIFYING EXPENSES AS DEPRECIATION

If a firm develops computer software for its business this year, it can depreciate this expense over a period. Alternatively, it could classify this expense as an operating expense, so that the entire expense is reported this year. If it depreciates the expense, it can spread the expense out over several years. The software development expense reported for this year would only be a small portion of the total software development expense. Therefore, this year's earnings will be inflated.

TIMELY WRITEOFFS

Firms in some industries have substantial flexibility to stretch expenses over time. Boeing spread its expenses to make its financial condition appear more attractive in 1997 when it merged with McDonnell Douglas Corp. Boeing's cost overruns on production were not completely divulged at the time because they were able to delay reporting some of the expenses until after the merger with McDonnell Douglas was completed. On October 22, 1998 Boeing announced that it would have a writeoff of $4.3 billion. The stock price declined by 20 percent over the next week. Some of the writeoff could have been taken in previous quarters when the cost overruns occurred. Since shareholders rely on the firm to disclose expenses, they were taken by surprise when Boeing announced the huge writeoff.

Boeing was hit with a securities fraud lawsuit by shareholders that it ultimately agreed to pay more than $90 million to settle. Some critics may argue that the accounting guidelines were at fault for the creative accounting used by Boeing. Others may suggest that Boeing's auditors were at fault for signing off on Boeing's financial reports.

CLASSIFYING EXPENSES DUE TO ACQUISITIONS

When a firm engages in acquisitions, its earnings can be substantially affected by the accounting method it uses when consolidating the two entities. Consider a firm that acquires another firm (called the target) for $500 million. The purchase results in a reduction of $500 million in its cash account. There must be offsetting entries to keep the balance sheet balanced. In general, the acquirer adds the book value of the target's assets to its own assets. The excess paid for the assets beyond the book value is called "goodwill," which is an intangible asset. That is, goodwill suggests that there is more value in the existing assets than their book value. If the acquirer paid $500 million for the assets, and it determines that the book value of the assets is $500 million, then the goodwill is zero. If these assets have a useful life of 4 years, accounting rules would allow the assets to be amortized by $125 million each year. This creates an expense to the firm of $125 million in the next 4 years, which will reduce the level of reported earnings.

Now consider how the annual expense reported by a firm can reduce the book value. Assume that it judges the assets to have a book value of $300 million, which means that the goodwill is $200 million. The depreciation on the book value of acquired assets would be $300 million over the 4-year period, or $75 million per year. Thus, if the firm judges its book value of acquired assets to be $300 million instead of $500 million, it can reduce its annual amortization expenses, and therefore boost its earnings. In the past, goodwill was also expensed (amortized) over time, but over a much longer period of time, and therefore at a slower pace. Consequently, there was an incentive to overestimate goodwill, because it resulted in a lower book value of acquired assets, a lower amortization expense, and therefore a higher level of reported earnings.

WorldCom used this deceptive accounting method after acquiring MCI. In 2000, it reduced the book value of its tangible assets that it acquired, thereby adding to the goodwill (intangible assets). This reclassification of assets enabled WorldCom to report lower annual depreciation expenses, which led to higher reported earnings. By some estimates, this accounting method inflated WorldCom's pre-tax earnings in 2000 by more than $600 million.

Recently, the accounting rules for goodwill have been changed. According to accounting rule FASB 142, firms must annually adjust their reported goodwill if they had initially overestimated it at the time of the acquisition. The firm must record that adjustment as a cost to completely reflect the degree to which the goodwill is overestimated. In essence, the accounting rules now require the goodwill to be written down immediately (rather than over a long-term period) when it reflects a permanent decline in value. Consequently, firms that overpaid on recent acquisitions may have large writeoffs, which will reduce the reported earnings. In essence, the large writeoffs within a single quarter may not necessarily be due to poor performance within that quarter, but to a previous acquisition. In the fourth quarter of 2002, AOL Time Warner took a one-time noncash charge (or writeoff) of $54 billion. While it may be unfair to interpret the charge as an expense of $54 billion in a single quarter, it is also dangerous to just ignore such a large writeoff. A portion of this huge writeoff is due to poor acquisition decisions.

Many other firms also had accumulated a large amount of goodwill from acquisitions, including WorldCom, Tyco, and Qwest. The goodwill must be written down to reflect the market values of the acquired units, which creates an expense for the firm. Some of the writeoffs were due to poor acquisitions that the firms made a few years earlier. Many of these firms used their highly priced stock as currency in the late 1990s to buy other companies. At the time, it seemed like they were buying companies for a reasonable price by providing their stock to owners of the acquired companies. However, these transactions flooded the market with their stock, which led to lower valuations of their stock.

Lack of Disclosure About Acquisitions

Shortly after the publicity about Enron's accounting, Tyco's accounting methods were questioned. Its financial statements were difficult to decipher because of the firm's many acquisitions. In February, 2002, Tyco International experienced a major decline in its stock price upon concerns about its account-ing methods. Tyco was publicly criticized because it had not disclosed some of the 600 acquisitions that it made during the 1999–2001 period. In addition, Tyco initially did not disclose that it paid $20 million to a director ($10 million to him and a $10 million donation to a charity he selected) for his services in an acquisition by Tyco. There were even allegations about its accounting of the acquisitions by some employees of the companies that it acquired. When investors became aware of this information, they sold the stock, causing the stock price to decline by more than 50 percent. The investor response was at least partially attributed to the uncertainty surrounding Tyco's financial condi-tion, and the lack of trust in Tyco's financial reporting.

Firms should disclose any loans provided to its executives. That money could have been used by the firm to serve shareholders rather than to serve the executives. WorldCom provided a loan of more than $400 million at a low interest rate to its CEO, so that he could pay off loans that he used to buy WorldCom stock. The stock price declined substantially after his investments, and he could not cover the debt payments. The loan from the firm to him is classified on the firm's balance sheet under "other assets."

DEFERRING CREDIT LOSS EXPENSES

In the summer of 2001, Providian Financial changed the manner in which it accounted for credit losses, which deferred about $30 million of credit losses into the third quarter. In this way, its pre-tax earnings during the sec-ond quarter were $30 million higher. The stock price was above $45 per share at the time. In July, one Providian executive sold a large amount of his Providian stock while another executive sold some of his stock options. Their actions occurred before the $30 million of credit losses was reported. The stock price declined once the credit losses were reported, and declined further to just $5 per share in October when Providian announced that its earnings would be weak. Some investors responded by filing lawsuits, alleging that the firm's executives inflated the earnings temporarily so that they could sell their options or shares at a higher price.

APPLYING GAINS TO REDUCE REPORTED EXPENSES

Accounting rules allow firms to account for gains from the sale of assets as a reduction in expenses, which creates the appearance of lower operating expenses. For example, in January, 2001, an IBM news release stated that its "selling, general, and administrative" expenses were reduced. It used an accounting method in which it classified the gains from sales on some assets as a reduction in expenses instead of revenue. When IBM was prompted by the SEC about this accounting method, it revised its accounting before submitting its 10K report to the Securities and Exchange Commission (SEC) in March, 2001.

CONSEQUENCE OF ACCOUNTING INDISCRETIONS

In recent years, there have been hundreds of cases in which firms were forced by the SEC to restate their earnings calculation methods. One of the most publicized cases involves Waste Management. Their earnings were overstated in the 1993–1996 period, which led to the SEC's action against Waste Management. Waste Management's restatement in 1998 corrected previous reported earnings by $1.4 billion. This adjustment was surpassed by WorldCom's earnings restatement to correct earnings over a five-quarter period by $3.85 billion.

While earnings restatements can ultimately correct the exaggerated earnings reports, they do not reimburse investors who were misled by the deceptive accounting practices. Many investors rely on the overstated earnings when they decide to purchase stock, and the stock price declines once it becomes obvious to the market that the earnings were exaggerated.

HOW ACCOUNTING CAN INFLATE GROWTH

WHEN INVESTORS EVALUATE recent earnings estimates in order to forecast future earnings or cash flow, they consider changes in economic conditions, industry conditions, and the firm's growth prospects. Even if two firms of the same size had the exact same financial performance last year, the firm with more favorable growth prospects will generally have higher expected earnings and cash flows and a higher valuation.

INFORMATION ABOUT GROWTH

A common source of information about a firm's growth prospects or efficiency is the summary provided by the firm's executives in the annual report, which can be obtained online or by contacting the firm. However, just as financial statements can be misleading, so can the statements made by firm's executives. Executives tend to be overly optimistic when discussing the firm's future prospects, which means that their statements must be interpreted with caution.

Enron provided the following information in its 2000 annual report:

- Enron has built unique and strong businesses that have limitless opportunities for growth.

- Enron is increasing earnings per share and continuing our strong return to shareholders.

- The company's total return to shareholders was 89% in 2000, compared with a –9% returned by the S&P 500.

- We plan to . . . create significant shareholder value for our shareholders.

Less than 1 year after Enron distributed this annual report, it filed for bankruptcy. Other companies that filed for bankruptcy, such as Global Crossing and WorldCom, also provided a very optimistic picture of their future in the annual reports they issued shortly before they filed for bankruptcy. While most annual reports do not contain such unrealistic expectations, they tend to offer a very positive outlook. Therefore, it is dangerous to develop estimates of a firm's growth or efficiency based on the firm's outlook for itself. Executives who oversee annual reports are not normally held accountable for an excessively optimistic outlook in the previous year. In fact, they may rationalize their unrealistic optimism by claiming that the annual report is more of a marketing tool than a reporting tool.

Investors do not have direct control over false promises or expectations, but they can at least recognize the potential for bias before blindly accepting the information provided in an annual report. Perhaps a reasonable starting point for determining the credibility of the firm's outlook in an annual report is a review of how accurate its outlook in previous annual reports has been. If a firm's annual reports over several recent years have had the consistent theme of "we had some problems this year, but everything looks favorable in the future," investors should be very cautious when interpreting the future outlook in the firm's current annual report.

ASSESSING THE SOURCE OF GROWTH

A commonly cited characteristic of some successful firms is their consistent growth in revenue over time. When a firm is able to grow its business at a rate that is consistently higher than the economic growth rate, it is usually because the firm has a good product line and good marketing skills.

Growth from Acquisitions

Many firms have grown mostly through acquisitions rather than by growing their own business. Acquisitions are not necessarily bad, as they can strengthen a firm's market share and may help the firm achieve more efficient production. However, be careful when assessing firms that have grown through acquisitions. When an acquisition occurs, the reported revenue, expenses, and earnings are consolidated on the income statement. Any revenue and earnings growth that results from combining two or more entities does not reflect the original firm's ability to grow its particular business. In other words, any firm can achieve growth in revenue or earnings every year if it can finance the acquisition of another company every year. But this type of growth does not necessarily enhance the value of the firm.

Growth from Intangible Assets

A firm's assets can be categorized as tangible assets and intangible assets. Tangible assets are assets that are visible, such as buildings and machinery. Firms with tangible assets can produce revenue-generating products with those assets. The potential productivity resulting from these assets is somewhat predictable, allowing for a more accurate valuation of the firm's assets.

Intangible assets include technology, patents, intellectual property, and the firm's reputation. These intangible assets can have a very high value. For example, a firm may have a patent that is valued highly, resulting in a high valuation for the firm's stock. However, there is more uncertainty surrounding the valuation of this kind of intangible asset. For example, the patent may generate substantial revenue for a biotechnology firm, but only for the few years before the patent rights expire and competitors are able to offer substitute products. Alternatively, some other types of technology may generate substantial revenue initially, but the revenue will quickly decline in future years as competitors match that type of technology. Again, the revenue that is currently being generated from this type of intangible asset will not continue indefinitely. Therefore, investors should be careful when using recently reported earnings generated by intangible assets to forecast future earnings or cash flows.

ASSESSING POTENTIAL GROWTH

When investors value a firm at a P/E ratio much higher than that of other related firms, the common reason is that the firm has higher growth prospects than other firms in the industry. However, investors should question unusually high P/E ratios. When firms experience strong growth during a period, they will not necessarily be capable of maintaining that growth rate. They may have had access to a technology that temporarily gave them a competitive advantage over other firms. However, competitors tend to monitor high-growth firms closely and to attempt to mimic the strategies that appear to have generated growth. That is, competitors attempt to mirror the business practices of the market leaders in order to gain market share. In addition, new firms will enter the market because they want to capitalize on the potential growth in the industry. While the industry leaders may hold their ground, they may not be able to maintain the growth rate that put them in the leading position.

Many firms that are industry leaders recognize that their growth may be limited. However, investors may have unusually high growth expectations for firms that have recently experienced high growth. Such optimistic sentiment about firms tends to cause an inflated stock price, which will ultimately be corrected.

C H A P T E R

7

HOW ACCOUNTING CAN REDUCE PERCEIVED RISK

FIRMS HAVE A NATURAL DESIRE to reduce the perception of their riskiness. First, when firms borrow money, there is the risk that they will default on the loans. They can obtain loans at a reasonable interest rate only if their financial condition is strong. One of the most common indicators of a firm's financial condition is its level of debt, since a high level of debt will require a high level of interest payments. A firm is more likely to default on its loans if it has an excessive amount of debt. If a firm can prove that its debt level is low, it can more easily obtain additional loans at low rates.

Second, a firm's stock may be valued more highly by investors if it is perceived to have a low level of risk. Investors are not as worried that the firm will go bankrupt.

Some firms have used deceptive strategies to reduce their amount of reported debt. In particular, they have used partnerships and leasing, which are explained in this chapter.

HOW PARTNERSHIPS CAN DISTORT RISK PERCEPTIONS

Many of the largest firms in the United States own partnerships. A partnership is structured differently from a corporation, in that its ownership is composed of partners, many of which may be managing the firm. In many cases, the ownership of partnerships and the accounting for them are sensible. In other cases, this action was primarily intended to disguise the firm's debt level and thus enhance the firm's value. Investors need to determine whether firms have created partnerships for practical business purposes or with the intention of manipulating their financial statements.

A firm may attempt to hide debt by creating a special partnership that will take part ownership of a portion of the firm's business. Some assets of the firm are transferred to the partnership, along with an equal amount of liabilities plus equity.

Suppose that a firm has $100 million in assets, which is supported with $60 million of borrowed funds (debt) and $40 million of equity. The debt ratio of this firm is

$$\text{Debt ratio} = \text{debt/total assets}$$

$$= \$60,000,000/\$100,000,000$$

$$= 60\%$$

Now assume that the firm converts some of its business into a special partnership. It allocates $40 million of assets and $30 million of debt to the partnership. The remainder of the firm now has $60 million in assets, supported by $30 million of debt. Now its debt ratio is

$$\text{Revised debt ratio} = \$60,000,000/\$30,000,000$$

$$= 50\%$$

This firm has lowered its debt ratio simply by moving a high proportion of its debt over to a partnership, and therefore removing that debt from its balance sheet. It has not changed its operations. It has reduced the reported debt on paper. Consequently, its debt appears to be reduced if investors focus only on the firm's financial statements and ignore the partnership's financial statements. Yet, if the partnership experiences financial problems, the firm may be obligated to the creditors of the partnership. It would be a mistake to ignore the partnership when assessing the firm's risk. However, investors who assess publicly traded firms commonly ignore partnerships for convenience or because insufficient information about the partnerships is disclosed.

The Enron scandal serves as a classic case of how partnerships were used to hide debt. Enron transferred some of its assets and liabilities to partnerships that it owned called *special-purpose entities (SPEs)*. It arranged a deal with other outside investors to invest at least 3 percent of the partnership's capital. When Enron created a partnership that would buy one of its business segments, it would book a gain on its consolidated financial statements from the sale of the asset to the partnership. In this way, the sale enhanced the income on its consolidated income statement. Enron had more than 800 partnerships.

Accounting guidelines allowed firms to exclude this type of partnership from its consolidated financial statements. Investors who focused on the consolidated financial statement did not recognize the amount of debt that Enron had.

Enron periodically booked losses from its partnership businesses on the partnership financial statements, while booking gains from its partnership businesses on its consolidated financial statements. On November 8, 2001, Enron announced that it would need to restate its earnings for the previous 5 years because three of its partnerships should have been included in the consolidated financial statements. There is a fine line between manipulating earnings within the accounting guidelines and violating the accounting guidelines. Enron crossed the line in its accounting for these three partnerships. Enron's previously reported earnings over the previous 5 years were reduced by about $600 million. The restatement confirmed that Enron's earnings had been inflated. However, by this time, the stock price had already plummeted, and many investors had lost most of their investment.

Looking back at Enron's financial statements, there were some hints of unusual partnerships that could be risky to Enron. For example, Enron's 2000 annual report mentions that Enron would have some obligations toward a partnership if its share price declined below a specific level. However, most investors, even those with an accounting background, would not have been able to recognize the potential risk with the limited information that was disclosed. Even if more stringent accounting guidelines for partnerships are enforced, there is still substantial flexibility in the reporting methods that may allow executives to disguise their firm's financial condition.

Since investors cannot control the lack of enforcement concerning accounting methods that are intended to disguise a firm's financial condition, they may attempt to learn enough accounting to monitor the firm's financial statements. However, even some accountants would have difficulty figuring out the financial condition of firms that own partnerships. In the case of

Enron, even many creditors who focus on assessing creditworthiness did not recognize the amount of Enron's debt. Enron's balance sheet showed debt of $13 billion, but when the debt contained within the partnerships was considered, the total debt may have been more than $20 billion.

Since the Enron scandal, investors have become concerned when they learn about some partnership relationships. When Adelphia Communications announced in March 2002 that it had loaned $2.3 billion to some of its partnerships, its stock price declined by more than 40 percent within 1 week.

HOW LEASING CAN DISTORT RISK PERCEPTIONS

Another method by which a firm reduces its perceived risk is to use leasing instead of debt. Consider a firm that needs a new manufacturing plant to produce many of its products. If the firm uses debt to finance its investment in the plant, it will incur large debt payments over the next several years. The high level of debt may increase the firm's risk, because it obligates the firm to generate enough cash flow to meet the periodic debt payments. A firm may be able to reduce the concerns of investors and creditors by leasing the plant instead of buying it. It would avoid the use of debt by making periodic lease payments to the owner of the plant in exchange for using the plant. Leasing expenses are a fixed periodic cash outflow, similar to that for debt. Yet, some investors will not recognize these expenses because they simply focus on the firm's debt. The accounting for leasing is not a gimmick, but investors need to recognize lease payments along with debt payments when estimating future fixed payment obligations.

8

HOW ACCOUNTING CAN CONTAMINATE YOUR INVESTMENT STRATEGIES

I F THE STOCK MARKET is "efficient," each stock should be properly priced, so that investors cannot develop a strategy that will achieve abnormal gains. That is, using a particular investment strategy to select stocks should not consistently result in better performance than just selecting stocks randomly. There are thousands of highly trained professionals who follow the stock market closely. These professionals include institutional investors who manage stock portfolios for mutual funds, insurance companies, and pension funds; advisers who recommend stocks for their clients; and stock analysts who monitor a specific set of stocks.

The fact that there are so many buyers and sellers of stocks at any given time indicates disagreement about the stocks' proper valuation. Investors who think that a stock is overvalued at a given price are selling it, while investors who think that the stock is undervalued at that same price are buying it. The price reflects a balance between the number of investors who thought the stock was overvalued and the number who thought it was undervalued. The fact that some investors have earned 50 percent or more during short periods of time suggests that stocks are sometimes wrongly priced. The potential for unusually high gains is what causes investors to pursue investments in specific stocks rather than investing in a conservative mutual fund. However, there is a downside to any strategy. Just as some investors guess correctly, others guess wrong and incur large losses as a result. Some of those bad guesses can be attributed to the wrong interpretation of financial statements.

EXPOSURE OF STRATEGIES TO ACCOUNTING PRACTICES

Many investors use investment strategies that are not focused on financial statements. Yet, their investment performance may still be affected by misleading accounting practices. Some of the more popular investment strategies are described here, along with their exposure to accounting practices.

Fundamental Strategy

Many investors monitor financial statements closely and attempt to identify undervalued stocks based on fundamentals (financial and other information). Given that this information is public, the prevailing stock prices should already reflect the information. Since this type of strategy relies on information that is available to all investors, it is likely to be effective only for those investors who have exceptional skills at interpreting financial information. Investors who rely on financial statements for the fundamentals may have a distorted perception of any firm whose financial statements were distorted by misleading accounting practices.

Contrarian Strategy

Some investors attempt to take a position opposite to the prevailing market sentiment. They buy stocks that have recently performed poorly and sell stocks that have performed well. This so-called contrarian strategy will be successful if the market sentiment tends to overreact to information and push the price too far in one direction. While there is substantial evidence of market overreaction during some periods, it is difficult to pinpoint when a stock's price trend will turn. The contrarian strategy does not rely directly on accounting information, but it can be influenced by accounting practices. When stock prices decline because of potential concerns about future earnings, a contrarian strategy may be to invest in these stocks. Yet, to the extent that the decline in value reflects suspicion about previous financial reports, this decline may be justified. Perhaps the price would have been much lower in the past if investors had interpreted the accounting properly. Thus, contrarian investors must attempt to distinguish those stocks that have a temporary low price from stocks whose prices will continue to decline. If they rely on the financial statements to make this distinction, they are subject to error as a result of misinterpreting the financial statements.

Relying on Stock "Experts"

Some investors rely on comments provided by so-called experts in magazines, on web sites, and on financial news networks. Some of these recommendations will pay off. Others will not. But there is no convincing evidence that acting on these recommendations will lead an investor to outperform the stock market in general.

When you buy a stock based on a recommendation, you are presuming that the adviser who provided the recommendation knows more than the market. Since a stock's price reflects the balance between investors who believe that a stock is overvalued and those who believe that it is undervalued, there must be other advisers who think the opposite of what your adviser thinks. Is your adviser smarter than the others? On any financial network, advisers gladly offer their recommendations, as doing so provides broad publicity for their firms. However, the advisers are rarely held accountable for their recommendations. Tomorrow, other advisers will be on the air offering a new set of recommendations. The focus is on hype rather than on accountability.

To the extent that advisers base their recommendations on fundamentals, they are subject to the same types of errors as other investors. Those advisers who can truly see through the financial statements may be capable of offering advice that can lead to abnormal returns for investors. Yet, research has shown that on average, financial experts do not beat the market in most periods. Individual investors should require more information about an adviser's stock-picking abilities before investing their money based on that adviser's recommendation.

INSIDER TRADING

Some research has shown that insiders (employees of a firm) are able to earn abnormally high profits from trading their employer's stock. Unfortunately, this places all of the outside investors at a disadvantage. While insiders have access to private information, other investors are at the mercy of trading by insiders. The insiders can sell their shares when they recognize financial problems at their firm that have not yet been publicized. Other investors will pay too much for the stock because they are unaware of the problems.

Insiders are not supposed to trade on the basis of material information that is not yet known to the public. The Securities and Exchange Commission (SEC) attempts to ensure that firms report accurate financial information, and that insiders of firms do not trade stock based on inside information that has not yet been disclosed to the public. Yet the SEC is limited in its ability to monitor all trades and prevent insider trading. There are more than 6000 stocks traded, and more than a million shares are traded per day for many of these stocks. It is impossible for the SEC to completely prevent insider trading. Investors should at least recognize that insiders sometimes use inside information to make trades or recommend trades to others. There are many cases in which insiders (or their relatives) have bought stock shortly before the firm announces favorable news or have sold stock shortly before the firm announces unfavorable news.

You can be at a major disadvantage relative to insiders when purchasing the stocks of smaller firms, because the amount of public information about those firms is very limited. Thus, the insiders have information beyond what the firm has publicly disclosed to the market. For example, the insiders may be aware that the firm's reported revenues are overstated or that its expenses are understated, even though its accounting process is within the acceptable guidelines. This inside information might cause insiders to dump the stock before other investors recognize the deficiencies.

The insiders may own a substantial percentage of a small firm's shares, and if they recognize that the firm is struggling financially, they may sell out before the news is made public. You can limit your exposure to such adverse effects by limiting the amount of funds you invest in stocks of small firms. Larger firms are not normally dominated by inside owners to the same degree as smaller firms, so the effects of insider selling on the stock price should be less pronounced.

Accounting Controls: Out of Control

C H A P T E R 9

WHY AUDITING MAY NOT PREVENT DECEPTIVE ACCOUNTING

FIRMS HIRE AUDITORS to ensure that their financial statements are within acceptable accounting guidelines. As already mentioned, a firm has some flexibility to use accounting methods that will temporarily inflate earnings. Yet, some firms have stretched this flexibility beyond the spirit in which it was intended. Auditors should impose some degree of control in these cases. However, auditors, like executives, are tempted to serve their own interests. Their compensation may be dependent on the amount of revenue that they generate. If they disallow some forms of creative accounting that may inflate a client's earnings, the client may hire someone else in the future. In addition, they may lose the consulting business that they were doing for that client. If the auditors sign off on misleading financial statements, investors cannot rely on those statements in valuing stocks. When an auditor receives large payments from a client, it does not automatically mean that the auditor has acted unethically. Large payments are paid for substantial services. However, there is a greater temptation for auditors to sign off on financial statements submitted by firms when the cost of not signing off (the amount of the forgone business) is high.

AUDITING XEROX CORPORATION

The fragile relationship between the auditor and the client can be illustrated with the case of Xerox Corporation. Xerox hired KPMG to audit its annual report for the years 1997 to 2000. In 2000, KPMG initially refused to sign off on the books because of some questionable reporting. In response, Xerox asked KPMG to change the manager of the audit team, and KPMG complied. Ultimately, KPMG did sign off on the audit in 2000, after requiring some restatements of previous financial reports by Xerox.

In 2001, the Securities and Exchange Commission (SEC) filed a complaint against Xerox because of its use of misleading accounting methods. The complaint was settled in 2002, with Xerox paying a $10 million fine. The SEC then initiated an investigation of KPMG's audit of Xerox, as it believed that KPMG was aware of some of the misleading accounting methods. KPMG earned a total of $62 million in fees from Xerox over the 1997–2000 period. Yet it argued that it was not aware of the misleading accounting methods that Xerox was using.

AUDITING ENRON

The conflict of interests for auditors became very obvious during the demise of Enron. Its questionable accounting methods did not prevent Arthur Andersen from signing off on the audit. In 2000, Arthur Andersen received $25 million in auditing fees from Enron, and an additional $27 million in consulting fees. Arthur Andersen knew that this business was contingent on its acceptance of Enron's accounting. Investors who relied on Arthur Andersen's validation of Enron's financial statements learned that they cannot necessarily trust audited financial statements.

Internally, some employees at Arthur Andersen questioned its endorsement of some of Enron's accounting methods. For example, a member of

Andersen's professional standards group objected to the accounting methods that were being used in 1999. Based on his suggested accounting method, there would have been a charge against earnings of at least $30 million. His objections were ignored, and he was ultimately removed from the professional standards group.

During the 1990s, the consulting side of the accounting business grew much faster than the auditing side. Accounting employees were given bonuses based on the amount of business they could generate. Auditing tasks commonly led to consulting business. But when an accounting firm does both auditing and consulting work for the same company, conflicts of interest are inevitable. An accounting firm does an audit of Firm M and establishes a business relationship with Firm M. Over time, Firm M requests extra consulting business, in addition to the audit. The accounting firm allows flexibility in the audit to ensure that it continues to receive Firm M's consulting business in the future.

AUDITING THE AUDITORS

As a result of the Enron scandal and other related scandals, auditors have received much negative publicity. Consequently, auditors recognize that they may be monitored more closely by the firm's board of directors, by the firm's investors, or by the SEC. They are thus more likely to ensure that firms stay within accounting guidelines. As a result, there should be fewer cases in which the auditors sign off on financial statements that blatantly violate existing accounting guidelines. However, this does not solve the problem of the deceptive accounting that can exist today. Firms can use deceptive accounting and still stay within the guidelines. To the extent that auditors focus simply on whether the accounting used by the firm is accurate, without focusing on what reporting method would make the most sense, deceptive accounting will continue. Consider the auditors as the police who are assigned to ensure that firms' accountants stay within the laws. Since the laws are loose, accountants can stretch their numbers without breaking the law. Some firms will report numbers that clearly reflect their business operations. Other firms will report numbers that are deceiving but within the rules. Both types of firms will be able to find auditors that will sign off on the financial statements. The auditors will not necessarily force the firms to change unless the accounting laws are changed to make firms report their financial condition more clearly.

10

WHY CREDIT RATING AGENCIES MAY NOT PREVENT DECEPTIVE ACCOUNTING

I NVESTORS COMMONLY rely on credit rating agencies for insight concerning a firm's risk level. Standard & Poor's (S&P), Moody's, and Fitch, Inc., are well-known credit rating agencies that rate various debt securities issued by firms that want to borrow funds. One potential advantage of credit ratings is that the agencies are not pressured to rate the firms excessively high, as they are not attempting to offer other services to the firms that they rate. Thus, credit rating agencies may serve as a useful monitor of firms that have financial problems. If investors cannot rely on a firm's accountants, auditors, or board of directors to ensure clear financial information, they can rely on credit rating agencies for ratings of the firms.

LIMITATIONS OF CREDIT RATING AGENCIES

Credit rating agencies do not always detect a firm's financial problems in advance. Enron was given a respectable credit rating by the agencies as late as 5 days before it filed for bankruptcy. Employees of the credit rating agencies explained that their rating was based on the information that they had, and that Enron had hidden some pertinent information about its partnerships from them. Congress deliberated about whether the credit rating agencies should be monitored. The agencies may have presumed that the firms were accurately reporting their accounting, or that the auditors were honest in their assessment of the financial statements. In order for the credit rating agencies to be responsible for determining whether the accounting numbers are accurate, they would have to do an audit themselves. If the accounting is faulty, no amount of credit analysts or regulators will detect a firm's financial problems well in advance.

Credit rating agencies have reduced the credit ratings of some firms when they became aware that the firms' accounting numbers were fictitious. However, since they tend to take the financial statements at face value, this adjustment in the rating occurs after the market has been informed of the faulty accounting. Thus, investors cannot rely on credit rating agencies to catch faulty accounting.

The credit rating agencies also did not recognize the amount of debt that Enron had. In October 2001, S&P affirmed a reasonably high rating for Enron, and provided an opinion that Enron's financial position should improve in the future. Within 2 months, Enron's debt rating was reduced to the lowest level. Credit rating agencies did not reduce Enron's debt rating until 5 days before it filed for bankruptcy. They also did not predict World-Com's bankruptcy. Perhaps the credit rating agencies, like investors, presumed that the financial statements were accurate.

A recent survey of firms by the Association of Financial Professionals determined that many firms do not agree with the ratings that they are assigned by credit rating agencies. A common criticism was that the ratings were not adjusted to reflect new information regarding the firm's risk. Some firms believe that the Securities and Exchange Commission (SEC) should allow other firms to enter the credit rating agency market, so that there would be more competition among credit rating agencies, which might lead to improved ratings. To the extent that the limitations of credit rating agencies are due to difficulties in interpreting financial statements, adding extra credit rating agencies will not solve the existing problem. If firms were forced to use similar accounting methods, the industry comparisons applied by credit rating agencies would be much easier and perhaps more effective. However, the credit rating agencies have no power to make the accounting regulators deal with the accounting guidelines.

Even if the credit rating agencies are effective at detecting bankruptcy in advance, their ratings cannot be converted into recommendations for investors. A firm with a high credit rating is not necessarily a good stock investment, because its stock may be expected to earn a very low return. There are many firms that have received the highest credit rating possible, but that have experienced poor stock performance over time. Therefore, stock investors should not rely on credit rating agencies for all of their stock decisions, even if they believe that the agencies can see through any accounting gimmicks.

11

WHY ANALYSTS MAY NOT PREVENT DECEPTIVE ACCOUNTING

SOME INVESTORS RELY ON STOCK ANALYSTS for opinions as to which firms' stocks are overvalued and which are undervalued. Analysts can provide a service for investors by offering ratings on each stock. There is evidence that in some cases, analysts have recognized a firm's problems before other investors in the stock market have done so. For example, a downgrade of a stock by a respected analyst often precedes a decline in the stock's price.

ROLE OF ANALYSTS EMPLOYED BY SECURITIES FIRMS

Stock analysts are commonly expected to have the skills and resources to see through deceptive accounting. Therefore, some investors rely on analysts' recommendations, so that they do not have to use their own time to determine which stocks are over- or undervalued. To the extent that analysts can see through deceptive accounting, they can steer investors to the firms whose favorable accounting numbers are truly warranted and away from those whose numbers are not.

However, analysts will not necessarily be able to detect a firm's deceptive accounting. Before Enron's financial problems were publicized, some of its employees joked that Enron's operations were frequently restructured simply to confuse stock analysts.

Furthermore, there is a conflict of interests that encourages analysts to provide biased ratings. Analysts who are employed by securities firms tend to assign high ratings to the firms that they rate. Low ratings could create negative publicity for the firms that they rate, and the employers of those analysts would lose business from those firms.

For example, if the analyst of Securities Firm Q rates Firm Z as a "sell," then Firm Z is not likely to consider hiring Securities Firm Q to help it with a possible merger or with a placement of new stock. Some analysts counter that they are under no pressure by their firm when assigning ratings. Yet, there are very few cases in which analysts employed by securities firms have assigned a "sell" rating to a firm that may potentially need consulting services. In the case of Enron, 16 of the 17 analysts who worked for securities firms rated Enron a strong buy before its problems were publicized. One analyst at a securities firm that was providing some consulting services for Enron downgraded Enron's stock in August 2001 (a few months before Enron's financial problems were publicized) and was fired shortly thereafter.

Some analysts employed by securities firms have received additional compensation when they helped the firm generate new business. For example, assume that Firm Y wants to issue more stock, but will issue new stock only if it believes that its stock will be in demand by investors. An analyst employed at Securities Firm S assigns a superior rating to the stock of Firm Y, which makes investors have more confidence in this stock. Consequently, Firm Y decides to issue additional stock. It hires Securities Firm S to conduct the stock offering in exchange for $3 million in fees. Securities Firm S passes on 1 percent of this amount, or $30,000, to its analyst in the form of an additional bonus for generating that business.

In this example, Securities Firm S did not order its employee analyst to assign superior ratings to all stocks. However, the securities firm did provide more compensation when the analyst generated business. The analyst knows that it is much easier to attract clients when potential clients have been given a superior rating.

The actual link between analyst compensation and the business generated by the analyst is not always direct. That is, an analyst's contract will not necessarily state that the compensation will equal a specified percentage of the business generated for the employer. However, the analysts that generate more business tend to receive higher compensation. In any case, it is difficult to imagine that an analyst would be highly compensated by the employer when assigning low ratings to many of the client's stocks.

Whether analysts assign inflated ratings to stocks because they are pressured to do so by their employers or because it is what they sincerely believe, their recommendations are of limited value. If you were at the racetrack, and the horse race expert stated that all the horses were excellent, the information would have no value. In the same manner, analysts' insight is limited if they view all stocks as great buys.

The Enron scandal illustrated the conflict of interests of analysts. The attorney general of New York and the Securities and Exchange Commission (SEC) initiated their own investigations of inflated ratings. For example, internal email messages by analysts were criticizing the very stocks that they were rating highly.

The conflicts of interest stretch beyond the relationship between analysts and the investment banking business. The volume of brokerage transactions can also be affected by analyst ratings, as investors may buy stocks because of the high ratings assigned to them. In addition, some securities firms have subsidiaries that manage stock portfolios (such as mutual funds) for individuals. Analysts may be hesitant to rate some stocks poorly if they are held by portfolio managers who work within the same organization.

NEW RULES FOR ANALYSTS

On May 8, 2002, the SEC announced new rules for analysts that have been phased in. These rules are intended to generate unbiased recommendations by analysts and remove some of the conflicts of interest that have caused biased recommendations in the past. A summary of the key changes is detailed here.

1. A securities firm that underwrites (sells) shares during an initial public offering (IPO) cannot report on that stock until 40 days after the IPO. This rule is intended to prevent the firm from using its analysts to promote the stocks it is selling. Historically, many IPOs have been complemented with favorable research reports by the analysts of the firms that served as underwriters. Critics argued that the analysts and underwriters were working together to place the stock, and that the analysts' research on the stock was biased.

2. Analysts cannot be supervised by the investment banking department within the securities firm. This rule is intended to separate the analyst perspective from the investment banking perspective. Analysts should assign ratings to stocks without concern about whether the ratings will generate business for the investment banking department.

3. Analyst compensation cannot be directly tied to business transactions, such as the number of deals that were the result of analyst ratings. This rule may allow analysts to rate a stock in an unbiased manner.

4. Analyst ratings must disclose information about the recent investment banking business (if any) that the analyst's firm has conducted for that firm, and about the analyst's ownership of the stock.

5. Analyst ratings must also disclose the meaning of each type of rating. For example, ratings such as underweight or moderate must be defined so that investors understand what the rating means. In addition, analyst ratings must also provide a summary of the proportion of its ratings that are in each rating class. Under the new rules, investors will be more aware of the grade inflation that exists. When analysts of a specific securities firm rate 95 percent of all stocks as a buy, investors should recognize that the rating is not very informative.

The rules may prevent some blatant conflicts of interest, but there are some conflicts that will still continue, regardless of the rules. First, even when analysts are completely separated from the investment banking department, their performance evaluation may still be affected by their ability to generate new clients for the securities firm. They are likely to be rewarded for generating more client business (even if there is not a specific formula in their contracts), which means that they still have an incentive to rate prospective clients highly. Moreover, most analysts will still not be willing to assign low ratings to stocks of large firms that frequently need investment banking services, because of the potential harm (lost business) to the investment banking department.

The only way to truly prevent the conflict of interest between investment bankers and analysts is to separate the ownership of the entities. Since such a separation is unlikely to occur, analyst ratings will still be biased upward. The new SEC rules are essentially enforcing disclosure that will help investors recognize that analyst ratings are biased. However, some investors still will not recognize the bias. They may think that the majority of ratings are high because the analysts provide ratings only for a select set of stocks that they truly believe in.

ROLE OF UNAFFILIATED ANALYSTS

Some analysts whose sole business is to rate stocks are not affiliated with a securities firm. Since they do not offer other services for the firms that they rate, they have no reason to provide biased ratings. These firms tend to have more sell recommendations than the affiliated analysts. However, even analysts without any bias may have difficulty rating firms that distort their financial statements. Until there are guidelines that force the accounting to reflect the firm's actual operations, the abilities of analysts are limited.

How Boards of Directors May Prevent Deceptive Accounting

12

BOARD CULTURE TO SERVE SHAREHOLDERS

A FIRM'S BOARD OF DIRECTORS is supposed to represent the share-holders. The board should recognize that deceptive accounting is detrimental to shareholders, and should prevent the firm from using deceptive accounting tactics that mislead investors. Any board member of any firm knows that the goal of a firm's board is to serve shareholders. But many boards do not serve shareholders. Board members may be tempted to approve corporate policies that serve the firm's executives or themselves rather than the firm's shareholders. Consequently, they may be willing to ignore deceptive accounting practices. The composition and compensation structure of the board determine the board's culture and influence the degree to which board members are willing to serve shareholders and prevent deceptive accounting.

INSIDE VERSUS INDEPENDENT BOARD MEMBERS

A board's culture is influenced by the self-interest of its members. Some boards are composed mostly of insiders who work for the firm. A board is more likely to focus on serving the firm's shareholders and ensuring proper accounting practices if there are independent board members serving on the board. Ideally, an independent board member, rather than the chief executive officer of the firm, should serve as chairman of the board. In addition, some boards encourage the independent members to meet alone, without the CEO or other inside members, after each board meeting, to ensure that any opinions by these members are communicated. Furthermore, a board should encourage its independent members to periodically meet with some executives or managers who are not on the board in order to obtain more insight into the firm's business. These efforts allow independent members to develop their own opinions about the firm without being completely influenced by the other board members.

CONFLICTS OF INTEREST DUE TO BOARD MEMBER COMPENSATION

There are different degrees of board "independence." Even if a board is stacked with independent members, it may still allow or even encourage deceptive accounting. Some board members are compensated in a manner that aligns their compensation with the short-term performance of the firm. If a firm uses fictitious accounting that inflates earnings and therefore inflates the firm's value in the short term, board members may benefit directly and allow such actions.

Board members of large companies earn about $150,000 per year for their work on the board. Some board members may be unwilling to question the accounting for fear that they might be removed from the board and their compensation would be discontinued.

Some independent board members receive consulting income from the firm, beyond the fees they receive for serving on the board. They may be tempted to please the executives rather than the shareholders so that they can retain their consulting relationship. Board members are likely to be more effective if they are not granted other consulting business by the firm. In addition, if they receive stock as compensation, they should be required to hold on to the stock for a long-term period, so that they will make decisions that will affect the firm's long-term performance.

While many board members may not have taken a board position with the intention of deceiving shareholders, they may lack the initiative to force a change in management behavior. A board member who is at odds with management will sometimes also be at odds with the rest of the board members, who have chosen to go along with management in order to keep their board seats. A board is likely to be more effective at serving share-holders if all its members truly have the same goal of serving shareholders. The easiest way to ensure that all board members have a unified goal is to ensure that their compensation from the firm is tied to the long-term value of the firm's stock.

LIMITED TIME AND ABILITIES OF INDEPENDENT MEMBERS

Not all independent board members are effective monitors of a firm's financial reporting. Some individuals serve on multiple boards and do not have the time to closely monitor each firm.

Other board members do not have the ability to properly monitor the firm's accounting, either because their experience is in another industry or because they do not have adequate accounting skills. It might seem that this deficiency could be solved by ensuring that all board members have accounting backgrounds. However, a basic understanding of accounting will not necessarily enable a board member to detect deceptive accounting practices. Board members may need actual experience in accounting work to recognize many types of deceptive accounting practices.

Yet, if the main focus of all board members were accounting, the board would forgo experience in other specializations, such as marketing, plan-ning, and human resource management. The board needs to understand accounting well enough to interpret the financial statements, but it should not forgo other specializations in order to ensure an adequate level of accounting experience. The ideal board composition may be a few board members who have extensive accounting experience and can serve on the audit committee (as explained next), while the other board members have other specializations. Such a diverse set of skills is effective for overseeing the firm's operations.

There are many board members who lack specific skills, but were placed on a board because they have good political connections. These members are unlikely to serve as good monitors of the business. In fact, they may be used by management to ensure that accounting regulations prevent or complicate adequate monitoring of a firm's accounting. Given their limited business skills, they may be even more willing to allow deceptive accounting (if they recognize it) because they may need the board position for their income or their ego. Their other career opportunities may be limited.

ROLE OF THE BOARD'S AUDIT COMMITTEE

Firms that have their stock listed on the American Stock Exchange, Nasdaq, or the New York Stock Exchange are required to have an independent audit committee that monitors the firm's auditors. The committee usually attempts to ensure that the audits are conducted properly, without any conflicts of interest. Consequently, if the audit committee members are truly serving as representatives of the shareholders, they should encourage the auditors to ensure that the financial statements are accurate.

The focus of the board's audit committee is likely to be on the auditors. Thus, the financial statements of the firm's accountants are audited by the auditors, who are monitored by the board's audit committee. The audit committee should consider direct communication with the firm's accountants to ensure that the accounting clearly represents the financial condition and operations of the firm.

Enron's Audit Committee

Some audit committee members may be tempted by their existing relationships with the firm to serve the firm's executives rather than its shareholders. Enron had an audit committee composed of six members. One member had a consulting contract with Enron that paid $72,000 per year. Two other members of this committee were employed by universities that received large donations from Enron. None of Enron's directors objected to Enron's accounting procedures during the 10 years prior to Enron's bankruptcy in 2001. The head of Enron's audit committee had previously been an accounting professor at Stanford, and clearly should have recognized that the procedures were questionable.

Separation of the Audit Committee from the Firm

The Sarbanes-Oxley Act of 2002 was created to prevent the types of conflicts of interest that existed within Enron's board. It mandated that members of the audit committee for the client firm should be on the board of directors, but should be independent of the client firm. They should not receive consulting or advising fees or other compensation from the firm beyond that earned from serving on the board.

Audit Committee Disclaimers

Recently, the biggest change regarding audit committees is that firms are adding more disclaimers to their annual reports, stating that the committees are not responsible if the audit is ultimately proved to be fraudulent. Thus, the creation of several checks to ensure proper accounting does not necessarily ensure ethical accounting if no one is held accountable for fraudulent accounting. In defense of the disclaimers, even some ethical audit committee members may be concerned that they will not necessarily catch a hidden conflict of interest between the auditor and the firm. A board member who serves on the audit committee normally receives a small amount of compensation for this extra board service. To many members, the reward for serving on the committee is not worth the risk, given the potential personal liability from missing some type of hidden conflict.

CHAPTER 13

BOARD MANDATE TO REVISE EXECUTIVE COMPENSATION STRUCTURE

EXECUTIVE COMPENSATION STANDARDS were substantially modified in the 1990s to eliminate some obvious conflicts between the interests of executives and the interests of the firm's owners. The new forms of executive compensation resolved some issues, but created others. The board of directors can implement compensation formulas that not only tie compensation to value, but discourage executives and managers from engaging in deceptive accounting or other unethical practices that will adversely affect value in the long run.

ALIGNING COMPENSATION WITH INVESTORS' GOALS

When the employees of a firm are not shareholders in the firm, they serve as agents who are responsible for serving the interests of the owners. A major concern of a firm's owners is that the employees will make self-serving decisions instead of serving the shareholders. If employees make decisions that serve themselves instead of the owners, the firm's revenue may be lower than expected. Alternatively, the firm may incur higher expenses if the employees use large expense accounts to fund their own personal lifestyles, or if the employees organize expensive conferences sponsored by the firm every quarter that have little impact on sales.

In the 1990s, firms started giving their employees incentives that were aligned with firm value. The incentives were intended to discourage employees from making business decisions in their own interests rather than in the interests of the firm itself and its owners. When employee compensation is tied to the value of the firm, employees may scale back unnecessary expenses that may reduce firm value.

STOCK OPTION STRUCTURE

There are many different ways of tying employee compensation to the firm's value. Firms with publicly traded stock often provide stock to their employees as part of their compensation. In some cases, stock options are provided, which allow employees to purchase the firm's stock at a specific price. Most executives of publicly traded firms have stock options.

Stock options have been used extensively to make sure that executives are making decisions that increase the firm's value. Consider an executive who is granted stock options allowing her to purchase 1 million shares of the firm's stock from the firm at $40 per share. If the stock is presently worth $43 per share, she could exercise the options by purchasing shares for $40, and then could sell the shares in the stock market for $43. She would have an immediate gain of $3 per share, or a total of $3,000,000 ($3 × 1,000,000 shares). If the stock price rises to $47, she could earn a gain of $7 per share, or $7,000,000, by exercising her option. Since her cost of purchasing the shares is fixed, her gain is directly tied to the price of the shares. If the stock price falls below $40, she would not exercise the option, because the cost would exceed the benefits. The structure of the stock options give her an incentive to make decisions that would enhance the firm's value, because her stock options will be worth more if the firm's value increases.

HOW COMPENSATION CAN ENCOURAGE EARNINGS MANIPULATION

A firm's managers are commonly evaluated on how they perform relative to competitors on various earnings performance measures. One common measure is the return on assets, which measures annual earnings as a percentage of the firm's assets. Since this ratio takes into account the size of the firm's assets, it can be used to compare the firm's earnings performance to that of other firms in the industry. An alternative proxy is the return on equity, which measures earnings as a percentage of the firm's equity.

Suppose you are the manager of a firm, and you have a choice to report your income in two ways. Your raise and the raises of all your subordinates are dependent on your firm's return on equity (ROE) relative to that of your competitors. An accounting method that most directly reflects your firm's operations results in an ROE of 16 percent. Alternatively, you could use a "generous" accounting method that will defer some of your expenses into next year, and therefore will result in an ROE of 22 percent. You prefer to use the more accurate accounting method. However, your main competitors use the more generous accounting method to determine their earnings, and their average ROE is 20 percent.

If you use the precise method, you and the other employees of your firm will be penalized, because your competitors will have achieved a higher ROE by applying a more generous method to derive their own earnings levels. Which accounting method would you use? Even the most ethical executives and managers would select the generous accounting method. If you and your employees are to be rated fairly, you need to use the same method as your competitors.

The implications go beyond employee compensation. Earnings measurements relative to competitors are commonly used by rating agencies, lenders, and analysts. No firm wants to be penalized simply because it provided a more precise measurement of its earnings.

One possible solution to this dilemma is for the firm's board of directors to identify other performance measures that are less susceptible to manipulation. However, this is easier said than done. Key measures of a firm's operations include revenue, expenses, and earnings, and all are subject to manipulation.

ADVERSE EFFECTS OF COMPENSATION PLANS

While these compensation plans have a well-intended objective of ensuring that managers focus on maximizing the firm's value, they frequently are ineffective at achieving their objective for the following reasons.

Short-Term Focus

Even if compensation plans effectively link compensation to a firm's stock price, they may not necessarily encourage executives to focus on the long term if they can successfully inflate the stock price for a short period. They can sell their holdings of the firm's shares at that time. This short-term manipulation is a disservice to investors who are investing in the firm over a longer time period. Consequently, the compensation plans may be a key reason behind the more blatant accounting abuses in recent years.

Enron serves as an excellent case in point. It granted stock options to its executives. By manipulating the financial statements, Enron consistently met its earnings forecast and achieved an increase in earnings over 20 consecutive quarters leading up to 2001. Investors valued Enron highly because of its earnings performance. Its financial statements misled investors and created an artificially high stock price while some executives sold their stock holdings. Before Enron's financial problems were recognized by the investment community, 29 Enron executives or board members had sold their holdings of Enron stock for more than $1 billion. In the 12 months before Enron's financial problems were publicized, its president, Ken Lay, cashed in stock worth about $77 million.

While executives do not have direct control over the stock's price, they do have control over their communication to investors about the firm's performance. They provide financial information to investors, which can have a strong influence on the demand for shares, the supply of shares for sale, and therefore the price of the stock. The value of shares is positively related to earnings, so overstated earnings may result in an overvalued stock. If executives are aware that earnings are overstated, they can exercise their options and sell their shares. They have an incentive to exaggerate the earnings so that the stock price is temporarily increased and they can sell their stock holdings at a high price. Once the public recognizes that the earnings were exaggerated, the stock price is likely to decline. Yet, by then, the executives have cashed out.

In January 2001, the chief executive officer of Oracle sold 29 million shares of Oracle stock. He also exercised stock options and earned a gain of more than $700 million. In the next month, Oracle announced that its earnings for the first quarter of 2001 would not meet expectations. Shareholders responded by suing the chief executive officer, alleging that he had timed his sales of shares in order to cash out before Oracle's weak earnings performance was disclosed to the public.

Weak Link between Options and Firm Performance

Stock options may not be properly aligned with the firm's performance. Again consider the firm that offers its executives options to buy its shares at $40. Assume that over the next year, the firm's stock price rises to $48, simply because of strong market conditions. An executive who has stock options to purchase 1 million shares will earn a gain of $8 million, even if the stock prices of all competing firms increased by a higher percentage over the year. That is, the executives are rewarded because of favorable market conditions, even though their firm performed poorly in comparison to its competitors.

In the late 1990s, stock prices soared, so that most stock options would have provided substantial benefits to executives, regardless of the firm's operating performance. One of the more extreme examples is the CEO at Qwest Communications, whose salary, bonus, long-term incentive pay, and money received from exercising stock options exceeded $100 million. In 2001, Qwest experienced negative earnings, and its stock price declined by about 75 percent over the year. Thus, the relationship between the firm's performance and executive pay is questionable in this example.

Conversely, a firm may perform well relative to its competitors, but its stock price could decline as a result of conditions over which the firm has no control. In this case, the executives may deserve more compensation than they receive. The traditional stock option structure does not account for general market forces, and therefore it has limited ability to align the compensation and the actual performance of a firm's executives.

Arbitrary Elimination of the Pay-Performance Alignment

If a firm's stock price declines, the value of the options that were granted declines, and the potential compensation for executives declines. However, some firms grant new options when old options become less valuable. This strategy eliminates the alignment between stock performance and pay when the firms perform poorly, as there is no penalty.

IMPROVING STOCK-BASED INCENTIVE PLANS

Stock-based incentive plans should be restructured to avoid the limitations described above. Improved plans have been implemented by some firms. Common revisions to improve the compensation plans are summarized next.

Set the Compensation Based on Relative Performance

Stock options should be structured to compensate executives only when the firm's performance is strong relative to that of competitors. The exercise price of the option could be revised each year to reflect the performance of competitors' stock. For example, if the firm's competitors experienced a 10 percent increase in stock price on average, the exercise price on the firm's options could be increased by 10 percent. In this way, executives holding the options benefit only if the firm's stock price increased by more than the 10 percent increase in the exercise price.

Limit the Amount of Options Exercised Per Period

Some stock options are structured so that the executives can exercise only a limited amount of their options in any period. This reduces the incentive for executives to inflate earnings in one particular period, because they can exercise only a limited number of options in any period. Stock options would be more effective if the gain were based on an average of the stock price over a particular time period. With this structure, there would be no incentive for executives to manipulate stock price for the purpose of timing the sale of their holdings of the firm's stock.

Restricted Stock

An alternative solution is to allocate restricted stock to executives and other employees. Normally, the stock is provided at no cost to employees. It is referred to as "restricted" because it is not usable until the employees satisfy specific vesting requirements, such as 5 years of service at the firm. The restricted stock for an executive may be allocated with staggered requirements, such as 10,000 shares provided after 3 years, 20,000 shares provided after 5 years, and 30,000 shares provided after 7 years. In 2003, Microsoft announced that it would use restricted stock as part of its compensation program. This created momentum for many other firms to consider switching from stock option compensation to restricted stock compensation. The benefits of restricted stock is that it forces executives to focus on maximizing the firm's performance over a longer time period.

14

BOARD MANDATE TO REPORT STOCK OPTION EXPENSES

BEYOND THE POTENTIAL TO ALIGN MANAGERIAL AND SHARE-HOLDERS' GOALS (if structured properly), the use of options enables firms to increase their reported earnings. Firms are allowed to ignore option compensation when they report their expenses on the income statement. A firm's board of directors can make the firm's financial statements more transparent by insisting that the option expenses be reported in the income statement.

POTENTIAL IMPACT OF OPTIONS ON REPORTED EARNINGS

Consider two firms, A and B, each of which has $90 million in revenue this year and has $50 million in all other expenses except wages and other compensation. Firm A pays its employees $30 million in annual wages, and does not offer stock options. Firm B pays no wages, but gives its employees stock options valued at $30 million. The pretax earnings reported by each firm are shown in Table 14-1.

Firm B reports higher earnings because its stock options do not have to be reported as an expense when reporting income. If investors use reported earnings as the basis for valuing stock, they will value Firm B higher than Firm A. Therefore, the use of stock options does not adversely affect Firm B's tax liability, while it enhances the firm's reported earnings. The stock option expense is typically reported in a footnote to the income statement.

Some firms argue that options should not be disclosed because this is not really an expense. That is, no cash is paid out, so there is no expense to the firm. Yet the granting of stock options does result in a cost to the firm. When a firm sells stock to its executives at $30 that could have been sold for $50 per share in the market, it receives $20 per share less than it would have received had it issued that stock to investors.

To illustrate this cost in another way, consider that many firms periodically repurchase stock to offset the new shares that are issued when stock options are exercised. The firm must pay the market price when it repurchases shares. Assume that stock options allow executives to purchase a total of 1 million shares of stock at $30. Also assume that the market price is $50 per share. If all stock options are exercised now, the firm is selling shares to the executives for $30 million (1 million shares × $30 per share) and then repurchasing shares in the market for $50 million. The difference is a cost of $20 million to the firm.

If stock options really were costless, firms would grant them to all employees, and even to all shareholders and charities. Firms most likely recognize that there is a cost to granting options but are concerned about how their reported earnings would be affected by including this expense on the income statement.

TABLE 14-1

	Firm A	Firm B
Revenue (in millions)	$90	$90
All expenses (in millions) except wages and stock option compensation	$50	$50
Wages (in millions)	$30	$0
Earnings before taxes	$10	$40

If firms had to report their stock options as an expense, the reported earnings of some firms would be substantially lower. In 2001, firms such as Disney, Intel, Microsoft, and Oracle made large payments as a result of providing stock option compensation.

Firms are allowed to deduct the cost of the options for tax purposes. They readily accept the argument that options are an expense for tax purposes, so they should also recognize options as an expense for reporting purposes.

There are different possible ways in which firms might expense the stock options. When other things are held constant, a rise in the stock price will result in higher expenses related to options, and will lower earnings. Some firms would prefer that the option expense not be accounted for on the income statement.

Some estimates suggest that the earnings of the S&P 500 companies would be 25 to 30 percent lower if the stock option expense were accounted for in the income statement. To the extent that investors already recognize the expense of stock options, the valuation should not be affected by how options are reported on financial statements. In other words, the price/earnings ratios of firms would be increased as the reported earnings were reduced by this adjustment, but the price would stay the same. Yet, the fact that some firms resist the proposal seems to suggest that they fear that investors do not recognize this expense. Consequently, a shift in this expense from a footnote to the income statement could cause a decline in reported earnings that is not completely anticipated by some investors. If the lower earnings triggered a sell-off of shares, it could lead to a lower stock price for firms. A lower stock price would possibly result in lower compensation for the executives who are granted stock options.

Some firms have taken the initiative and included the stock option expense on the income statement. Boeing and Winn-Dixie accounted for options in their income statements in 2002, while Amazon.com, Bank One, The Coca Cola Company, and Washington Post announced that they would disclose the option expense in their income statements in 2003. However, many firms may avoid accounting for this expense on the income statement until they are forced to do so.

ROLE OF THE BOARD IN DEVISING AN OPTIONS PLAN

A firm's board of directors is responsible for devising a system that will tie compensation to the firm's long-term performance. In 2000 (the year before Enron went bankrupt), Enron's board approved $750 million in cash bonuses to Enron's executives. In addition, it approved a credit line for the president, Ken Lay, of $7.5 million, which he could repay with his stock. Many firms still use faulty compensation structures. Some board members are compensated in a way that is similar to that used for the executives, and therefore they may prefer that the existing structure continue so that they can benefit personally.

15

BOARD EFFORTS TO TAME CORPORATE EXECUTIVES

ONE REASON THAT FIRMS USE DECEPTIVE ACCOUNTING is to hide managerial inefficiencies. That is, the accounting is a means of making investors believe that the firm's financial condition is stronger than it is. Many executive and management inefficiencies take the form of excessive spending. When firms generate more cash than they need to cover expenses, the excess is sometimes referred to as free cash flow. A disadvantage to a firm of having free cash flow is that the firm's executives and managers may use the cash to benefit themselves rather than the shareholders. Under these conditions, they may be tempted to disguise their accounting to satisfy existing or potential shareholders.

To the extent that a board of directors can prevent excessive spending by executives and managers, they may reduce the temptation for executives to use deceptive accounting. There would be no need for a firm to provide deceptive financial statements if the honest facts would satisfy investors. A board of directors may be able to prevent excessive spending by (1) initiating or increasing dividends, (2) using debt financing, (3) allowing the firm to become a takeover target, and (4) monitoring.

INITIATE OR INCREASE DIVIDENDS

Since dividends represent cash outflows, they reduce the net cash flows that are available to the firm's managers. Thus, they can effectively discipline the managers' spending and may reduce waste. Since firms that pay dividends may have less excess cash, they may be less likely to waste funds. Conversely, firms that pay zero dividends may have more flexibility to use cash in ways that serve the managers more than the shareholders.

Dividends can also limit deceptive accounting by providing more information about the firm's cash flow situation. A firm would plan to provide dividends of $.20 per share per quarter only if it expects to have sufficient cash to make the quarterly dividend payment. Thus, the dividend payment may indicate the minimum amount of cash that the firm should generate in each quarter after paying normal operating expenses.

Furthermore, dividends may limit the potential deceptive accounting of shifting a portion of the normal operating expenses to nonrecurring expenses. If firms use their cash to pay dividends, they may not have enough cash to engage in acquisitions, and therefore they may not pursue acquisitions. Consequently, they will not be expected to have nonrecurring expenses and will not be able to hide normal operating expenses in this way.

However, investors should not presume that a firm's accounting is transparent just because the firm pays dividends. Many firms that pay dividends still engage in acquisitions. Even if they have less cash, they may finance the acquisition by borrowing funds or by using their stock as a means of purchasing a target. Therefore, they will have some nonrecurring expenses from the acquisitions and may attempt to shift some normal operating expenses there. Even if the dividends prevent them from making acquisitions, there are other accounting methods that will allow them to hide some normal operating expenses or to inflate revenue.

Enron, Dynegy, Xerox, WorldCom, and Waste Management paid dividends, and yet had to engage in earnings restatements because they inflated their reported earnings. While the dividends may indicate the forecasted minimum level of cash that is available to a firm after paying operating expenses, they do not accurately indicate the level of earnings.

Granted, zero-dividend firms usually have more flexibility to waste cash, but these firms should not necessarily be viewed as inefficient just because they do not pay dividends. Firms that are planning for high growth need funding, and they may be better off investing their cash in their own growth rather than distributing dividends (assuming that they are investing their funds in feasible projects). While dividends may restrict potential waste, they also restrict the potential benefits that could be achieved if the firm were allowed to invest more funds in its expansion.

USE DEBT FINANCING

Just as dividends can reduce free cash flow and reduce waste, so can debt. A firm that has periodic debt payments must be disciplined and use its cash properly so that it can make its debt payments. Debt is even more restrictive than dividends, because the creditors can force a firm into bankruptcy if it does not meet its debt obligations.

A firm may signal its future cash flows when it decides to use debt financing. It would consider borrowing funds only if it expects to generate sufficient cash flows to cover its debt payments. Thus, its financial situation may be more transparent if it uses debt.

However, investors should not presume that a firm's accounting is transparent just because the firm has a substantial amount of debt financing. In fact, firms that use debt financing may be enticed to inflate their reported revenue or deflate their reported expenses so that they can more easily qualify for credit. While investors may feel more secure knowing that a firm is being periodically monitored by its creditors, there have been many cases (such as Enron and WorldCom) in which creditors were not able to detect a firm's financial problems before the problems were made public.

Low-debt firms may have more flexibility to waste cash, but low-debt firms should not necessarily be viewed as inefficient just because they have more cash to spend. Firms that are planning for high growth need funding, and they may have less exposure to cash flow problems if they fund some of their expansion with equity rather than debt.

ALLOW THE FIRM TO BECOME A TARGET

The market for corporate control implies that weak firms are vulnerable to a possible takeover by stronger firms. A board may be able to prevent deceptive accounting and other unethical practices by allowing the firm to become a target that another firm can acquire. Such a strategy may force the firm's executives to make decisions that serve its shareholders. If the firm's executives make poor decisions, another firm (called a raider) may be able to buy the firm cheap, get rid of the ineffective executives, and improve the firm. The raider benefits because it should be able to increase the value of this business by buying it cheap and improving it over time. Thus, a firm's executives are supposed to be concerned that if they do not satisfy shareholders, they will be replaced. If a firm's executives do not manage a firm properly and attempt faulty accounting gimmicks, they will be subject to the market for corporate control.

If the market for corporate control works, how do we explain the bankruptcies of Enron, Global Crossing, and many other firms? Why didn't a raider acquire them and turn them around? First, the board may be unwilling to allow a firm to become a target. Board members might lose their positions if the firm is acquired.

Second, consider the raider's intentions: (1) Buy a weak firm at a low price, and (2) replace executives of that firm who are not doing their jobs. If the firm used deceptive accounting to inflate its earnings, it also has an inflated stock price. This type of firm is not appealing to raiders because it is valued too high by the market. Raiders are unwilling to acquire a weak firm at an unusually high price. Third, removing executives can be very expensive. These executives may have contracts that provide them with substantial compensation if they are fired. Fourth, the weak firm may have some hidden liabilities that are not so obvious. In the case of Enron, raiders could have been liable for various claims made by Enron employees or business partners that Enron cheated them. Given the limitations described here, deceptive accounting and unethical behavior by a firm's executives are not necessarily prevented by the market for corporate control.

IMPROVE MONITORING

Executives and other managers commonly engage in activities that are not in the best interests of their shareholders. In some cases, the boards of directors approve these activities even though they are not in the best interests of shareholders. In other cases, the directors are not informed about the activities, either because they chose not to be or because they did not monitor the firm's executives and managers as closely as is necessary.

The following examples illustrate various unethical activities that were not prevented by the board of directors. The founder and CEO of Adelphia Communications financed much of his own country club's expenses with Adelphia's funds. The CEO's family used Adelphia's assets as collateral for their personal loans. In addition, the family invested in Adelphia stock with borrowed funds, but when the stock declined, it used more than $250 million of Adelphia's funds to cover loan obligations. In June 2002, Adelphia filed for bankruptcy.

Tyco International used hundreds of millions of dollars to provide some of its executives with a wide variety of perks, including loans, homes, and apartments. In 1998, the CEO (Dennis Kozlowski) used a $19 million loan from Tyco with a zero percent interest rate to pay for a home. In 2000, the loan was forgiven as a bonus for Kozlowski, and more than $10 million of Tyco funds was used to furnish an apartment in New York. In 2001, Tyco paid more than $1 million for a birthday party for Kozlowski's wife on the Italian island of Sardinia. Tyco funds were also used to help finance Kozlowski's art and antiques, an estate in Nantucket, and a yacht. There were many smaller examples of excessive spending financed by Tyco, including $110,000 for a 13-day trip to London and $6000 for a shower curtain. The perks were publicized after Kozlowski and the chief financial officer (Mark Swartz) were indicted on charges of corruption, conspiracy, and grand larceny.

In the 2000–2002 period, WorldCom's compensation committee (a subset of the board of directors) approved loans to Bernie Ebbers, the CEO. The committee was concerned that Ebbers would sell his personal holdings of WorldCom stock to cover many of his personal loans, which could have caused the market price of the stock to decline. The total amount granted to Ebbers exceeded $400 million.

There are many other examples in which firms' use of cash is not as blatantly unethical, but is just as costly to shareholders. One of the most common examples is when executives and other managers pursue growth through acquisitions. Some acquisition efforts are rational because they combine entities that can help each other (synergy). However, many acquisitions lack rational motivation or are not properly executed. There is substantial evidence that acquisitions commonly reduce the value of the acquiring firm (although there are some exceptions). Acquisitions can backfire when the acquiring firm's business is unrelated to that of the target, when the merging of the two businesses causes conflict and bad morale, or when the acquiring firm pays an excessive premium for the target.

A board of directors oversees a firm's decision to engage in acquisitions. Thus, its approval of a bad acquisition suggests either that it is unable to recognize bad acquisitions or that it simply signs off on whatever executives want to pursue, without doing its own analysis.

The complete effect of an acquisition cannot be assessed until several years later, and even then it is difficult to isolate its effect on the firm's value. By the time it is recognized that the acquisition was a mistake, the firm is involved in other acquisitions or projects, and there is no penalty for the managers who were involved in decisions that were made years earlier. The only penalty is imposed on the shareholders in the form of an abnormally low stock price.

It is difficult to determine whether the poor use of cash by some executives and other managers is the result of unethical behavior or incompetence. In many cases, the desire to grow probably overshadows concerns about potential integration or morale problems associated with merging two businesses. There are no laws that prevent poorly motivated acquisitions or other managerial decisions regarding the use of cash. Thus, investors will continue to be subjected to poor managerial decisions that are intended to benefit the managers rather than the investors who own the firm's stock. A board of directors cannot be held responsible for preventing all bad acquisitions. But it can at least determine whether a proper assessment of the potential benefits and costs of an acquisition has been conducted. It should also consider the potential effects on shareholders before approving the firm's proposed acquisitions.

How Governance May Prevent Deceptive Accounting

16

GOVERNANCE BY THE FINANCIAL ACCOUNTING STANDARDS BOARD

IN GENERAL, FIRMS ARE MOST LIKELY TO PROVIDE TRANSPARENT FINANCIAL STATEMENTS if there are clear, standardized rules that do not allow creativity. Accounting should be a means of accurately disclosing a firm's financial condition, not a strategy that can be used to hide its financial condition. The Financial Accounting Standards Board has the power to set narrow guidelines. In addition, the Securities and Exchange Commission (SEC) and the stock exchanges can serve as enforcers if firms do not abide by standardized accounting guidelines. However, the Financial Standards Accounting Board still allows substantial accounting flexibility, which allows firms to be overly creative. This flexibility prevents clear comparisons of financial information between firms and complicates the valuation process used by investors.

REQUIRE STRICT ACCOUNTING GUIDELINES

Using honest accounting puts firms at a disadvantage relative to competitors that use deceptive accounting within the broad accounting rules. That is, the firm's performance might look worse than that of its competitors if it uses more transparent accounting methods rather than whatever methods are standard for the industry. This dilemma will continue as long as accounting guidelines allow firms to be creative. If the accounting guidelines were standardized, firms would be forced to report financial information that would be more directly comparable.

Accounting rules could be revised to limit a firm's flexibility in reporting its firm's financial condition. That is, an operating expense would have to be counted as an operating expense, and could not be hidden. A one-time capital gain could not be counted as revenue. Accounting rules could be more influential in leading to accurate disclosure of a firm's financial situation. Narrower guidelines would lead to more complete disclosure in the financial statements.

Proposals for standardized guidelines for deriving pro forma operating earnings have been made. The Financial Accounting Standards Board has been unwilling to enforce standardized accounting guidelines. It appears that efforts to standardize accounting guidelines are caught within a maze of divergent interests, which may stall or dilute any revisions.

THE USE OF CORE EARNINGS FOR STANDARDIZED REPORTING

Standard & Poor's has taken the initiative to encourage more standardized reporting, even though it does not have direct control over the accounting guidelines. It has devised a standardized measure of earnings, which it refers to as core earnings. The main adjustments made to derive core earnings are (1) to count employee stock options as an expense, (2) to exclude pension gains from earnings, and (3) to include restructuring charges as an expense. As argued in the previous chapter, employee stock options should be recognized as an expense. Whether executives deserve the money or not, the firm incurs an expense when it provides this form of compensation, and so should report it. Pension gains do not result from the firm's operations and therefore do not serve as an indicator of the firm's existing or future operating performance. Therefore, they are not considered to be core earnings.

When a firm incurs expenses as a result of restructuring, those expenses are real and should not be ignored. Some firms seem to have restructuring charges almost every quarter, so it is dangerous to assume that some form of restructuring charges will not occur in the future.

Since core earnings include some expenses that firms prefer to overlook when they report their earnings and exclude pension gains, they will be lower than the typical earnings measure used by most firms. Consequently, the ratio of share price to earnings (P/E ratio) will increase when core earnings are used. Some critics suggest that the use of core earnings could scare investors by making them think that the prevailing stock price is too high. However, many investors normally reassess the reported earnings by making the same adjustments that are used to derive core earnings. The core earnings measure should not be hidden from investors just because it provides a more honest and less favorable measurement of operating earnings. Furthermore, if investors prefer other measures of earnings, they can ignore the core earnings.

The use of core earnings does not eliminate the need for thorough analysis of financial statements, but it might make the analysis a little easier. Differences in industry characteristics would still cause earnings to be different across industries. Yet, investors can compare core earnings adjusted for size among firms within an industry. In this way, they can capture the unique industry characteristics while comparing a more accurate indicator of earnings than the firms typically provide.

17

GOVERNANCE BY THE SEC

T HE SECURITIES ACT OF 1933 attempted to ensure complete disclosure of relevant financial information on publicly offered securities and prevent fraudulent trading of securities. The Securities Exchange Act of 1934 identified deceptive practices that were illegal, such as misleading financial statements and trading strategies designed to manipulate the market price. In addition, it led to the creation of the Securities and Exchange Commission (SEC). As a result of the 1933 and 1934 legislation, the SEC was given the responsibility for monitoring the stock exchanges and publicly traded companies. It requires those companies that are listed on an exchange to file a registration statement and financial reports with the SEC and the exchanges. This requirement is part of a larger goal: to ensure that firms fully disclose any information that could affect the value of their stock or of other securities that they have issued. By ensuring complete disclosure, these acts attempt to prevent some investors from having an unfair advantage over other investors because of their access to inside information.

ORGANIZATION OF THE SEC

The SEC has five commissioners, who are appointed by the President of the United States and confirmed by the Senate. Each commissioner serves a 5-year term, and the commissioners' terms are staggered. Each year, one commissioner's term comes to an end, and a new one is added.

The commissioners meet to make broad decisions about the regulations. They can also set assignments for employees of the SEC. They have the power to revise regulations, but some revisions may require congressional review.

The SEC is organized into divisions, and several divisions have responsibility for overseeing stock market participants and transactions. The Division of Corporate Finance assesses the registration statement issued when a firm goes public, and also other financial reports. It attempts to ensure that firms fully disclose all pertinent financial information to existing or prospective investors. However, the SEC has not had sufficient resources to closely and continuously monitor firms' financial reporting. The SEC is not expected to duplicate the work performed by the public accounting firms that serve as auditors. Furthermore, the SEC is not empowered to force firms to use the accounting method that would provide the most transparent information about its performance or financial condition. Firms have substantial freedom to be creative when determining how to measure some expenses and revenues.

The Division of Market Regulation monitors the actual trading of securities. It attempts to ensure that trades are executed at the proper prices, without collusion among the organizations that execute trades for their customers.

The Division of Enforcement is responsible for taking action against individuals or firms that have violated specific guidelines. It may investigate suspicions of insider trading by assessing stock transactions. It may file a case in federal court, or even join other federal agencies to prosecute individuals for criminal activity in stock markets.

The Sarbanes-Oxley Act, implemented in August 2002, increases the SEC's budget and enables it to enforce rules related to financial disclosure more effectively. Some of the more important means by which the SEC is attempting to ensure more accurate and ethical financial reporting are summarized here.

HOLDING EXECUTIVES AND DIRECTORS ACCOUNTABLE

Some critics suggest that the accountability for fraud should start with the firm's managers and directors. If these individuals were held fully accountable, they would be discouraged from deceptive reporting. Managers and directors have rarely gone to jail for fraud of any type. In some cases in which they were subject to a fine, the fine was an insignificant portion of their wealth. Managers commonly use corporate funds to hire defense attorneys (another cost to the investors). Even if managers are convicted, various state laws (such as those of Florida and Texas) allow them to protect a large amount of their assets. The criminal justice system is not likely to prevent corporate fraud.

Tougher criminal prosecution would not discourage faulty accounting unless the accounting standards were tightened to prevent abuse. That is, there are legal ways to manipulate accounting, and firms can use any method of accounting that falls within the flexible guidelines, even if it misleads investors. For example, the use of an unusual accounting method that is intended to inflate earnings and therefore to inflate the firm's value might not be considered fraud as long as the method is within accounting guidelines.

One major concern about imposing tougher laws is that while it could discourage fraud, it may intimidate some ethical managers or board members. Consider a board member who is truly attempting to ensure that the firm's managers serve shareholders' interests. Many board members are not experts in accounting. While they can attempt to ensure that accounting does not mislead investors, it is unfair to make them liable for the actions of the firm's accountants or auditors. It is difficult to impose laws that discourage the disreputable directors without scaring away those who are ethical.

HOLDING THE CEO ACCOUNTABLE

A related idea is to require that any financial report include the CEO's signature as a personal guarantee of the financial statement's accuracy. In the past, some CEOs have suggested that they were completely unaware of the fraudulent accounting within their firm. In the case of Enron, the CEO

(Kenneth Lay) claimed to have no knowledge of faulty financial reporting, even after the $1.2 billion writeoff that Enron announced on October 16, 2001. Would those CEOs make such claims if they had to sign off on financial statements?

The Sarbanes-Oxley Act attempted to ensure the accountability of the CEO and CFO. CEOs and CFOs of very large firms must certify that the firm's financial statements are accurate. Thus, this SEC rule makes the CEOs and the CFOs more directly accountable for the reliability of financial statements.

However, consider a firm that has several executives who own substantial numbers of shares of the firm's stock. If these executives anticipate that the firm's performance is beginning to decline, they may attempt to inflate revenue or earnings in the near future to keep the stock price high and then sell their shares. The CEO could become liable without really playing a role in the unethical behavior.

A counter to this argument is that a CEO could hire an independent consultant to ensure that the financial statements provide complete and accurate disclosure before he or she signs off on them. Of course, this is one reason firms have auditors and a board of directors in the first place. The CEO's independent auditor may be able to ensure the accuracy of financial statements only by conducting a complete audit, which is already being done officially by the independent auditors.

Furthermore, there is a difference between ensuring the financial statements' accuracy and preventing the firm from misleading investors. The CEO's independent auditor could ensure that the financial statements are technically accurate, but if they are later found to be misleading because relevant information was left out, the CEO who signed off on the statements could still be liable. It is natural for even ethical CEOs to be concerned about the concept of personally guaranteeing complete and accurate disclosure in financial statements. The clarity and accuracy of the statements may vary with one's perspective, because of the high degree of subjectivity when applying accounting rules.

SEPARATING AUDITING FROM NONAUDIT CONSULTING

Many investors have argued for a separation between the firm that serves as auditor and the firm that provides nonaudit consulting. On average, auditing firms earn more money from nonaudit fees from their audit clients than they do from their audit work. For example, in 2000, Arthur Andersen earned $25 million from Enron for auditing and $27 for nonaudit consulting. The separation of audit and nonaudit consulting would limit the leverage that the firm has over the auditor. Perhaps the temptation to secure future business would be reduced if the potential business was limited to audit work only.

In 2000, the SEC proposed that accounting firms provide auditing or consulting services, but not both types of services. Several accounting firms and the American Institute of Certified Public Accountants (AICPA) lobbied members of Congress against the SEC's proposal. There were strong objections to the proposal by 52 members of Congress; 20 of these members were on the Energy and Commerce Committee, and 6 were on the Financial Services Committee. Many of these members of Congress received donations from the accounting lobby. The chairman of the Senate's banking committee (which oversees the funding for the SEC) received about $200,000 in contributions from the accounting lobby over the 1995–2000 period. Overall, the members of Congress who wrote letters to the SEC objecting to the proposal received more than $3.5 million from the accounting lobby. Some of these same members later expressed their outrage about Arthur Andersen's audit of Enron and the conflict of interest between Arthur Andersen's audit and the consulting business it did for Enron.

The Sarbanes-Oxley Act of 2002 required that any nonaudit services performed by a public accounting firm for a client firm for which the accounting firm is auditor be approved by the client firm's audit committee. It also prevents a partner's compensation from being tied to the amount of nonauditing services sold to a client.

REQUIRING FAIR DISCLOSURE BY FIRMS

Regulations are imposed by the SEC and the stock exchanges to prevent actions that would allow some investors an unfair advantage over others. Firms listed on stock exchanges in the United States must file a registration statement and financial information with the SEC and the exchanges. In doing this, firms must disclose any information that could affect the values of the securities that they issue. In addition, the SEC requires that all investors have the same access to information. In the past, even with these requirements, firms would commonly divulge pertinent information to stock analysts, who could then advise their larger clients based on the information. The larger institutional investors may have had an advantage over individual investors.

In 2000, the Securities and Exchange Commission introduced a new regulation called Fair Disclosure (Reg FD) to ensure that all investors have equal access to financial information about firms. Reg FD requires firms to disclose all relevant information to all investors at the same time. It is intended to ensure that a firm does not leak information to specific parties before it announces the information to the market as a whole. It was enacted in response to allegations that firms would commonly feed information to stock analysts (who assign a rating to the firm's stock) before they disclosed that information to the entire market. The analysts, who commonly work for investment banks, might then leak the information to institutional investors, which are favored customers of the investment banks. The result of such leaked information is that some investors may have an unfair advantage over others because of their access to information.

Any information about a firm's operations that could affect its value (stock price) must be broadly disseminated through a public news release or on the firm's web site. Firms may still have conference calls with analysts, but the information that they consider relevant should have been disseminated broadly before the call. Individual investors are now allowed to listen in on many conference calls.

Given that analysts can no longer rely on inside information from firms, they may rely more heavily on financial statements. Yet, to the extent that the financial statements can be manipulated to inflate earnings, even assessments of firms from reputable analysts are subject to significant errors.

CHAPTER 18

GOVERNANCE ENFORCED BY THE SARBANES-OXLEY ACT

T HE GOVERNMENT CAN ENACT LAWS TO CONTROL REPORTING PRACTICES and penalize abuse. Historically, government employees have their own special interests, which conflict with serving individual investors. Members of Congress have had ample opportunities to change the laws in a manner that would prevent some accounting abuses. Yet, they have passed on these opportunities. Many of them have received campaign contributions from the accounting agencies and used their power to prevent any change in accounting practices.

The publicity surrounding the accounting scandals forced Congress to take action. The Sarbanes-Oxley Act was enacted in August 2002. This act improves the governance over the accounting process and should help to prevent blatant abuses of accounting and auditing ethics. However, it will not necessarily prevent the more common and subtle forms of misleading accounting that are conducted within the loose accounting rules that firms are allowed to use. Some of the provisions of the act were mentioned in previous chapters. Since this act may have a profound effect on financial reporting by firms, it deserves additional attention here. Details of the act are summarized on many web sites, including that of the American Institute of Certified Public Accountants (AICPA).

KEY PROVISIONS

Some of the key provisions of the act are provided here.

Public Company Accounting Oversight Board

A public accounting oversight board is created to ensure ethical auditing practices. Specifically, the board is assigned to register public accounting firms, conduct inspections of accounting firms, conduct investigations of accounting firms, and impose sanctions when necessary to penalize accounting firms for abuses. The board also ensures independence of the audit from the client who hires the audit. Each accounting firm is required to register with the oversight board and maintain records about their audit work for 7 years. Each public accounting firm pays an annual fee, and will be assessed by the board every 1 to 3 years.

There are five financially literate members, each of whom serves on a full-time basis for the Public Company Accounting Oversight Board for a period of 5 years. Two of the members must be or have been certified public accountants, and the other three members may not be certified public accountants.

Comments   While more oversight appears to be needed, is another government agency necessary? Couldn't the Securities and Exchange Commission (SEC) perform these functions if given sufficient resources? There may be some inefficiencies and power struggles in the coordination between the SEC and the Public Company Accounting Oversight Board that could have been avoided if the SEC were allowed to perform these functions.

Commission Oversight of the Board

The SEC is responsible for overseeing the board. It can inspect the board's records. The board must notify the SEC of investigations and may coordinate the investigations with the help of the SEC's division of enforcement.

Comments   The auditor ensures that the firm is doing its job properly, the firm's board and the Public Company Accounting Oversight Board ensure that the auditor is doing its job properly, and the SEC ensures that the Public Company Accounting Oversight Board is doing its job properly. If accounting rules were more objective and less subject to manipulation, financial statements would be more transparent, and all this oversight could be minimized.

Nonaudit Services

A public accounting firm is only allowed to provide non-audit services when auditing a client if the client's audit committee pre-approves these services before the audit begins. The committee must disclose this pre-approval to investors.

Comments   This provision may help to prevent the obvious conflicts of interest that have occurred in the past. Yet, it is surprising that such a provision was not implemented 70 years ago when other regulations were implemented to prevent conflicts of interest that could distort information and adversely affect investors. It took a case of massive fraud by Enron, one of the largest firms in the world, to get the attention of lawmakers. Furthermore, preapproval by a client's audit committee does not necessarily prevent the temptation for public accounting firms to sign off on the audit in exchange for the extra nonauditing work.

Compensation for Nonaudit Services

Partners in charge of an audit can not be compensated based on the amount of non-auditing services that are sold to a client.

Comments   This provision may prevent the blatant conflict of interest that occurs when a public accounting firm signs off on the audit in exchange for additional nonaudit services. However, partners of accounting firms will still be compensated on the basis of how much business they generate, just like partners of many service firms. Thus, they will still be indirectly compensated on the basis of the amount of nonauditing services that they sell. However, this is not a problem if they are truly held accountable for performing a legitimate audit.

Rotation of Partners Who Oversee an Audit

The top two partners who oversee an audit must rotate off the audit every five years, and must wait five more years before returning to audit that client.

Comments   This provision is intended to separate the relationship between partner and client firm so that the audit is performed in a legitimate manner.

Conflicts of Interest

The client firm's CEO, CFO, or other employees in similar roles may not have been employed by the public accounting firm in the one-year period prior to the audit.

Comments   This provision may also prevent some blatant conflicts of interest, but it is surprising that this law did not already exist.

Audit Committee

The members of the audit committee for the client firm should be on the board of directors, but independent of the client firm. That is, they should not receive consulting or advising fees or other compensation beyond that earned from serving on the board from the firm.

Comments   This provision can help prevent blatant abuses in which the auditors signed off on financial statements that were misleading.

Corporate Responsibility

The CEO and CFO must certify that the audited statements fairly represent the operations and financial condition of the firm.

Comments   Do we need a law that makes the chief financial officer and the chief executive officer responsible for the financial reports that are disclosed by their firm? If a production manager is responsible for the products sold to the market, why wouldn't the chief financial officer be responsible for the financial information provided to the market? The CEO and CFO should have always known that they were responsible for financial reports, but if this provision prevents them from pretending that they did not have such responsibilities, then it may be effective.

Manipulation of Auditors

> It is unlawful for an officer or a director to manipulate or mislead auditors in a manner that may create a misleading audit.

Comments   Do we need a law beyond existing laws that make it unlawful for an officer or director to mislead auditors? Is this action any different from a firm's lying about the contents of its products that are sold to customers? Existing laws that hold firms accountable to their customers apparently do not hold firms accountable to their investors.

Reimbursement of Executive Bonuses due to Restatements

> If a firm is forced to provide a restatement because its initial financial reports were misleading, its CEO and CFO are required to reimburse the firm for any bonus or incentive-based compensation that they received as a result of the misleading reports.

Comments   Do we need a law beyond existing laws to enforce this provision? This provision appears to say that if any officers earn extra compensation due to manipulating financial statements, they must give the money back. Does this imply that in previous cases, executives convicted for manipulating financial statements for their own personal gain before the law are not required to reimburse the firm?

Insider Trades

> Officers and directors are not allowed to purchase or sell stock during designated black-out periods (periods in which specific employees who may have some inside information about the firm are not allowed to trade the firm's stock). If such trades occur, any profits from these trades may be confiscated.

Comments   This provision seems to imply that before this law, it was acceptable for officers and directors to purchase or sell stock during blackout periods. If so, who were the blackout periods directed toward in the past? Is there anyone in the firm who would have greater access to inside information than officers and directors?

Disclosure

Each financial report must be consistent with GAAP guidelines.

Each annual and quarterly report shall disclose all material off-balance sheet transactions and other relationships with unconsolidated entities.

Comments This provision seems to imply that before this law, it was acceptable for accountants to make up whatever guidelines they wanted for financial reporting.

SEC Resources

The SEC is granted a larger budget so that it can more effectively ensure proper and timely reporting of financial condition or performance by firms.

Comments This provision is needed so that more effort can be applied to enforcing the existing laws rather than rewriting laws that in spirit already existed.

Intent to Hide Evidence

Actions that are intended to hide evidence are subject to a fine or imprisonment.

Comments So before this provision, one apparently could hide evidence that shows how investors were cheated out of billions of dollars, and such actions would not be subject to punishment?

Intent to Impair Evidence

It is a crime to alter, destroy, mutilate, or conceal any document with the intent to impair the document's use in official proceedings.

Comments Is there no existing law that makes it illegal to conceal evidence? Was it necessary to include so many verbs here? Can an officer "purposely misplace" a document, since such an action may not be construed as concealing or mutilating?

CONCLUSION

The provisions of the act essentially seem to impose some barriers that prevent a conflict of interest for auditors, officers, or board members, and to state that if these parties engage in unethical actions, they will be punished.

Perhaps the act will be effective in discouraging officers, board members, and auditors from using fraudulent reporting practices. However, the act does not focus on accounting guidelines. To the extent that firms can misrepresent their financial condition by using creative accounting that is within the loose guidelines, it may be difficult to prove that such reports are fraudulent. While the act may discourage blatant abuses, it may not prevent the more common and subtle abuses, such as exaggerating earnings by shifting some normal operating expenses over to "nonrecurring expenses" in order to inflate operating earnings. Such subtle abuses occur frequently, and they will be prevented only if accounting standards are narrowed to make firms use accounting that truly reflects their operations. As it stands, the rules are lenient, and it is rational for firms to make their numbers look as good as their competitors' within the rules that have been set.

19

GOVERNANCE BY STOCK EXCHANGES

S tock exchanges enforce rules that may prevent firms from engaging in deceptive accounting or unethical forms of financial disclosure to investors.

BACKGROUND ON ORGANIZED STOCK EXCHANGES

Stock markets can be classified according to whether they provide a visible marketplace. An organized exchange is a visible marketplace for secondary-market transactions. Examples of organized exchanges include the New York Stock Exchange, the American Stock Exchange, and the Midwest Stock Exchange. Trading on the New York Stock Exchange (NYSE), the largest organized stock exchange, accounts for about 80 percent of the value of all organized stock exchange transactions in the United States. More than 3000 firms have their stock listed on the NYSE. Many large firms that have widely traded stocks are listed on the NYSE.

Each organized stock exchange has a trading floor where designated participants (called floor traders) execute transactions for their clients. To be eligible to execute stock transactions, individuals must purchase a seat on the stock exchange or work for someone who does and must have the proper certifications to trade stocks. There are 1366 seats on the NYSE, and the only way someone can buy a seat today is if one of the existing owners of a seat is willing to sell it. The price of a seat has ranged between $1 million and $2.3 million over the last 8 years.

Each stock transaction on an organized exchange represents the sale of existing stock by one investor to another investor. Thus, the exchange serves the secondary market for stocks.

When customers submit orders to brokerage firms, these orders are sent electronically to floor traders on an organized exchange. Floor traders may be employees of a specific brokerage firm, or they may be independent and serve various brokerage firms that need transactions executed.

Floor traders stand in a specific area of the trading floor if they want to trade a particular stock. In trading stock, an auction process is used. When they sell a stock for a customer, the floor traders attempt to sell the stock at the highest possible price. That is, they announce to other floor traders that they want to sell a specified number of shares, and then they sell the shares to the highest bidder. When they purchase a stock for a customer, they attempt to obtain the stock at the lowest price possible. However, most of the trading occurs quickly, without negotiations. Floor traders are aware of the price at which they may be able to buy or sell a stock because they know the price at which the most recent transaction involving that stock occurred. Transactions in widely traded stocks occur continuously throughout the day. A number of floor traders are attempting to buy or sell the stock at the same time, and the general demand and supply conditions dictate the price at which the stock will be traded. If conditions for a stock are favorable, many customer orders to buy the stock will be submitted to brokerage firms and relayed to floor traders. Yet, there will not be many customer orders to sell that stock under these conditions. Therefore, the stock's price will rise because the demand for the stock exceeds the amount of stock that is for sale.

If conditions for a stock are unfavorable (for example, if its earnings are lower than expected), many customer orders to sell the stock will be submitted to brokerage firms and relayed to floor traders. Yet, there will not be many customer orders to buy that stock under these conditions. Therefore, the stock's price will decline because the amount of stock for sale exceeds the amount of stock that is demanded.

Many transactions on the NYSE are executed by computer, not by individuals on the trading floor. Small trades on the NYSE are executed through SuperDot, which is an electronic system for matching up buy and sell orders on the NYSE.

HOW TRADING IS INFLUENCED BY ACCOUNTING

Buy and sell orders determine the demand for a stock and the supply of shares for sale on a particular exchange. The orders may be triggered by information concerning a firm's performance. The information about a firm is frequently derived from a firm's financial reports. Thus, to the extent that the financial reports are misleading, they can cause misinterpretations that lead to buy or sell orders. Therefore, they can cause a stock's price to deviate from its proper value.

LISTING REQUIREMENTS

Organized stock exchanges specify requirements that firms must meet in order to have their stocks listed there. For example, the NYSE requires a specified minimum number of shares of stock outstanding. When there is a large number of shares, there is more active trading. Consequently, the stock is more liquid, which means that it can be easily traded at any time. The NYSE wants to ensure that its stocks are liquid, so that anyone who wants to buy or sell the stocks can do so quickly. Liquid stocks are monitored and traded by more investors. There is less of a chance that false information could cause misvaluations of stocks, because there are more informed investors who can correct any mispricing that occurs. However, the cases of Enron and WorldCom showed that even widely traded stocks are subject to wrong valuations. When faulty accounting information has been provided and most or all investors believe it, the prices of liquid stocks can deviate far from their proper values.

In addition to the requirement for a minimum number of shares, the NYSE also requires that the listing firm generate a specified minimum level of revenue over a recent period. Small firms are unable to meet this requirement, and therefore are not eligible to list their stock on the NYSE. This requirement ensures that only the larger stocks are traded on the

NYSE, but it does not necessarily prevent accounting fraud. Other organized stock exchanges also have listing requirements for their firms. However, these requirements are not as stringent as those of the NYSE.

A firm can be delisted by an exchange for not having enough independent members on the audit committee, for not providing an annual report, or for not complying with annual shareholder meeting requirements. In general, the exchanges have not been stringent about enforcing these requirements. However, they imposed additional guidelines following the Enron scandal. Additional enforcement may help limit the potential damage from faulty accounting. But additional enforcement by exchanges will not necessarily catch faulty accounting.

OVER-THE-COUNTER MARKET

In addition to the organized stock exchanges, the over-the-counter (OTC) market also facilitates stock transactions in the secondary market. In the OTC market, a telecommunications network is used to execute the transactions instead of a trading floor.

A popular system that serves a portion of the OTC market is the National Association of Securities Dealers Automatic Quotations (Nasdaq), which facilitates electronic quotations and trading. More than 5000 stocks trade on the Nasdaq, including some very well-known technology stocks such as Intel. However, most stocks listed in the Nasdaq market are relatively small firms, as the listing requirements are not so stringent. Some stocks traded on the OTC market are thinly (infrequently) traded and are not as closely monitored by investors. These stocks are more susceptible to faulty accounting because there is less oversight by investors.

Another system that serves a portion of the OTC market is the OTC Bulletin Board. Its listing requirements are very liberal. It lists stocks that have a price below $1 per share. More than 3000 stocks are listed here. The stocks that are traded within this system are often referred to as penny stocks. They are less liquid than stocks that are traded on other exchanges. Some of these stocks are not traded at all on many days. There is very limited information about these stocks, so investors may be forced to rely almost exclusively on any financial information that the firms disclose. Thus, the valuations are highly susceptible to error, since the financial reports could be misleading.

AFTER-HOURS TRADING

For stocks that are listed on the NYSE, American Stock Exchange, and Nasdaq market, there is now an after-hours trading session. This session allows investors to trade stocks after the normal trading hours. Most of the trading occurs in the 90 minutes following the close of normal hours or in the 90 minutes prior to the opening of normal trading hours. Some information about profits is disclosed by firms at night (after normal trading hours), and some investors trade after hours in order to capitalize on the information before other traders trade on it during normal hours. However, the volume of trading after hours is limited. Therefore, one or more large orders can move a stock's price substantially during the late trading session, and cause the price to deviate far from its proper value. Investors may be more capable of buying or selling shares at a fair price during normal trading hours than at night, because there is a larger number of investors who can attempt to process any new information that is provided.

REGULATION OF STOCK TRADING

Beyond the listing requirements mentioned earlier, stock exchanges impose other requirements to ensure that firms disclose sufficient information to investors. Stock markets are regulated by stock exchanges to protect the investors who invest in stocks. In general, the regulations are intended to ensure that investors are not placed at a disadvantage when buying or selling stocks. The NYSE uses a computerized system and personnel to monitor the trading behavior on the trading floor.

Stock exchanges attempt to prevent insider trading, in which a trade is based on information that has not been disclosed to the public. For example, if executives of a biotechnology company have just learned that one of the company's experimental drugs has been approved by the Food and Drug Administration (FDA), they may want to buy more shares of the firm's stock before the news becomes public. By doing so, they would obtain the shares at a relatively low price. This act represents insider trading. The executives would buy shares from some other investor at a price that does not yet reflect the information that they have. The investor who sold the shares without knowing this information has been cheated.

Regulations that prevent insider trading can prevent one investor from having an unfair advantage over another investor. These regulations are critical for building the trust of investors who participate in the stock markets.

In some cases, the insiders have access to unfavorable information and attempt to sell their shares before other investors are aware of that information. This strategy allows them to sell their shares at a higher price. Yet, the investors who purchase their shares are at a disadvantage, because they did not have access to that information. A classic case of insider trading occurred when ImClone's ex-CEO Sam Waksal learned of unfavorable information (the FDA's rejection of a new drug created by ImClone) and warned family members to sell the stock. According to prosecutors, family members sold about $9 million of ImClone stock at that time. Martha Stewart sold shares at about the same time. Since she was a friend of Waksal's, her actions led to a government investigation to determine whether she used inside information. This insider trading case demonstrates how insiders may benefit at the expense of other investors.

While regulations against insider trading have good intentions, they do not prevent some forms of insider trading. For example, many executives of firms sold holdings of their company's stock in the 2001–2002 period, before the stock price declined. In some cases, the firm's financial statements did not fully disclose the negative conditions that prevailed at the firm. It appears that the executives were able to sell their stock at a higher price because they had inside information about the firm that was not obvious from the financial reports. That is, the financial reports may have caused many investors to value the stock at a much higher price than it deserved. This allowed the executives to sell their shares of the firm's stock at a higher price. The executives who sold their shares benefited at the expense of the buyers of these shares.

Regulations do not ensure that stocks will perform well and do not prevent irrational or incompetent investment decisions. They simply attempt to ensure that investors have equal access to information when making their investment decisions. Moreover, they do not prevent losses that occur because of fraudulent accounting. The stock exchanges are not effective in preventing firms from being creative within the loose accounting standards in order to exaggerate earnings.

REQUIRING MORE INDEPENDENT DIRECTORS

In June 2002, the New York Stock Exchange proposed additional requirements for firms listing stock there, including the following:

- The board's compensation committee, which establishes compensation methods for executives, should be composed only of outside directors, who are not employed by the firm.

- Stockholders are allowed to vote on the firm's stock option compensation plans.

- The audit committee of the board (the committee that oversees the audit process) is composed only of outside directors, who are not employed by the firm.

- The audit committee has the power to fire an independent auditor.

- Any nonaudit work by an independent auditor must be approved by the audit committee.

If the firms do not follow these requirements, the New York Stock Exchange could impose penalties, including delisting the firm's stock from the exchange.

DOES THE NYSE GOVERN ITSELF?

The NYSE may have lost some credibility as a corporate governance enforcer when it was announced in August 2003, that its chariman, Richard Grasso, would be receiving $140 million in deferred compensation. Then in September, the NYSE announced that Grasso was entitled to an additional $48 million. Grasso decided not to accept the additional $48 million after listening to the objections of some the exchange's board members. Many critics questioned the corporate governance guidelines that the NYSE used for determining compensation. The information about Grasso's compensation even shocked some of the NYSE's board members.

V

How Investors Can Cope with Deceptive Accounting

20

LOOK BEYOND EARNINGS

AS MENTIONED EARLIER, valuations are commonly based on earnings estimates. Thus, it is not surprising that executives might be tempted to manipulate earnings in order to increase the value of their firm's stock. In particular, investors tend to respond strongly to any information that may alter the prevailing quarterly earnings trend.

If investors could truly derive an accurate forecast of earnings into the distant future, they could properly value stocks. Unfortunately, earnings are subject to much uncertainty, causing any valuation based on expected earnings to be questionable. Many investors have limited time and insufficient skills to develop an accurate forecast of long-term earnings, and therefore they rely excessively on this quarter's earnings as the key indicator of the firm's future earnings. Since firms want to please investors, they feed the investors' short-term earnings addiction. In essence, the investors' addiction is transmitted to the firm's managers who are responsible for pleasing investors. Until firms cure their addiction to short-term earnings, investors need to cure their own addiction by understanding the business.

UNDERSTAND THE BUSINESS

If investors have the time and the skills, they may be able to derive a better valuation of stocks by looking beyond the earnings. They can more properly judge whether to trust a long-term earnings forecast if they understand the business behind the earnings. An understanding of a specific business can trigger some concerns or suspicions about earnings forecasts, allowing investors to recognize when earnings estimates are misleading. For example, if investors had applied some business concepts to the telecommunications industry during the bullish period in the late 1990s, they would have recognized that it would be virtually impossible for all telecommunications firms to experience the type of growth that some firms and analysts were predicting. Many new firms entered the industry, and a shakeout was inevitable, even if the industry growth had continued. Furthermore, the entrance of new competition was bound to cause more competitive pricing, which would reduce the profit margins of all firms. These basic business concepts were ignored by many investors, who focused completely on attaching valuations to earnings forecasts rather than questioning the earnings forecasts.

There is no valuation model that can derive a precise valuation of a stock when inaccurate earnings are used as input. An understanding of a firm's business does not guarantee an accurate estimate of the firm's earnings, but it may at least help investors avoid some stocks whose earnings are suspect. Many investors who do not have the time to truly understand a firm's business rely on analysts for the valuation. But if analysts focus only on the earnings numbers without really understanding the business, this does not solve the problem. Therefore, investors should consider the following checklist of basic business concepts before investing in any stock.

Mission and Strategic Plan

What is the firm's mission statement? Normally, the mission is broad, but it can be considered when determining whether the firm is focused on its mission.

What is the firm's strategic plan? Some firms establish strategic plans that deviate from their original mission when the prospects in their industry are limited or when competition is fierce. Such a strategy may be rational if the firm has the core competencies and the vision to deviate from its original mission effectively. However, if it is just shifting its business as a means of growth without focus, it is likely to flounder. When firms grow through a series of unrelated acquisitions (as Sunbeam and Tyco did), investors should question the future direction of the firm. Growth for the sake of growth can lead to costly acquisitions that disrupt the company's core operations.

Outlook

• Does the firm have the potential to grow?

• What is the firm's outlook?

• Is there reason to believe that the firm can achieve its goals?

When using an annual report to obtain information about a firm's outlook, there is an art to extracting that information. Most businesses (even the efficient ones) are trained to use a positive tone when communicating information. Thus, the term *excellence* shows up in many mission statements, whether the firm is excellent or is failing. Some firms seem to spend more time on self-promotion than on achieving what they promise in the annual reports. Thus, investors should be cautious about using the annual report to obtain information and should not be influenced by the glowing remarks provided by the firm's investor relations person or communications person, who was assigned to ensure that the annual report promotes the firm in its most positive light.

Any firm is likely to defend its self-promoting tendencies by arguing that all other firms do it, and that a lack of exaggerated self-promotion would put it at a competitive disadvantage relative to other firms. Of course, this is the same argument that is made by firms who use creative accounting to exaggerate their earnings. To the extent that investors focus on facts rather than hype, the valuation of the firm's stock should not be influenced by the number of times that the firm uses such terms as *excellence, growth strategies*, and *efficiencies*.

If you skim through numerous annual reports, you will notice that a firm's outlook is typically more positive than its recent performance. Next year is always going to be better than this year. Such optimism is part of the culture, like a New Year's resolution at the corporate level. Executives may be naïve eternal optimists, or they may believe that investors are gullible enough to believe it. Before you trust the firm's outlook, at least look back at the previous annual reports to determine whether its outlook in previous years turned out to be accurate.

Firms commonly justify their acquisitions by arguing that they will extract synergies from the combination of businesses or that they will be able to reduce their average costs by eliminating redundant operations of the combined businesses. Yet, many firms do not ever achieve the expected cost efficiencies that they projected as a result of the acquisition. Whether the executives of firms are wrong because they are naïvely optimistic or because they fabricated a reason so that they could build bigger empires through costly acquisitions, their promises of shareholder benefits that will result from an acquisition fall short. In many cases, their compensation increases following an acquisition, even if the acquisition has an adverse effect on the value of the firm. Thus, there is good reason for investors to question this form of growth, even if there is no hidden agenda involving the use of an acquisition as a means of reducing the reported expenses.

Exposure to the Economy

How sensitive is the firm's performance to economic conditions? If a recession occurs, by how much will its sales decline? Can it survive a recession? Does it have substantial fixed costs that will still exist even if sales decline? Economic conditions are difficult to forecast. Yet, investors should at least be able to recognize how exposed a firm is to economic conditions. At the very least, they can assess how the firm performed during the last period in which economic conditions were weak.

Exposure to Industry Conditions

How sensitive is the firm to industry conditions? Is there a chance that regulations will increase, which could cause additional expenses? Is there a chance that regulations may be reduced, which may increase competition? Are there particular industry characteristics (such as asbestos) that are likely to result in lawsuits against the firm?

Exposure to Global Conditions

How sensitive is the firm's performance to global conditions? Is it subject to foreign competition? Could foreign firms with lower expenses penetrate the market and pull market share away from the firm? Is the firm's performance sensitive to a change in exchange rates?

Management

A firm's performance is highly influenced by its key decision makers. An understanding of the backgrounds, structure, and incentives of management can help determine whether the decision makers have the skills and incentives to make good decisions.

Background of Managers

- What is the background of the firm's top managers?
- How long have they been employed by the firm?
- How much experience do they have in the industry?

For a fast-growing firm that is growing in different directions, a danger signal may be the hiring of many executives who do not have much background in the industries that the firm has targeted for growth.

Organizational Structure

- What is the firm's organizational structure?
- Does the firm have several layers of managers?
- What is the average cost per employee?
- What is the ratio of total salaries to total assets?

An excessive number of layers of management may reflect inefficiencies. The ratio of total salaries to total assets will vary among industries, but it can be compared within an industry. A high ratio suggests excessive costs relative to assets. An alternative ratio is salaries to sales, which may more directly measure the cost-effectiveness of the firm's revenue generation.

Management Turnover

- Does the firm have a high turnover rate?

A high turnover of executives in a firm that appears to have been successful recently should trigger suspicion. The turnover may signal negative prospects that are known to the executives but are not yet known to investors. At the very least, it deserves a closer look.

Management Compensation Structure

- What is the firm's compensation structure?
- Have the top executives earned unusually high compensation even in years in which the firm performed poorly?

If the compensation structure allows high compensation regardless of the firm's performance, it may not provide the necessary incentives for executives. Even if accounting numbers tell the truth in the future, a firm's executives may not have an incentive to achieve high performance if their compensation is not properly tied to performance.

Production Costs

- What is the nature of the firm's production?

- Does it need a consistently high sales level to cover a high level of fixed costs? Does it benefit from economies of scale?

- Can its production costs be reduced in periods during which sales decline?

Inventory Control

- Is the firm able to maintain sufficient inventory?

- Does it frequently need to lower prices in order to dump excessive inventory?

Quality Control

- Does the firm differentiate its product from competitors' through quality or in some other way?

- What is the firm's reputation for quality?

- Is there any chance that the firm's sales level will decline because of quality concerns? Is the quality level dependent on one key supplier?

Marketing

- Is the firm's performance sensitive to its marketing strategy?

- What is the firm's channel of distribution from its production to the customer?

- Does the firm rely on intermediaries? If so, what is its relationship with these intermediaries? Is there any chance that it will lose business in the future because the intermediaries push the competitors' products?

- Does the firm have the potential to increase its product line?

- Does the firm rely on patents and research and development for growth? Does it need to spend substantial funds on marketing just to maintain its market share?

Finance

- How does the firm finance its business? Does it rely heavily on debt?

- If so, is there any concern that the firm will not be able to meet its future debt payments?

- What is the cost of the firm's debt?

- If the firm's sales decline in the future, can it still afford to cover its debt payments?

- Does the firm have too much stock issued to the public?

- Does it periodically repurchase some of its shares? How does it use its retained earnings?

Governance

Are the firm's managers focused on maximizing the wealth of shareholders? If the firm has a proper governance structure, its managers are more likely to be serving shareholder interests. Consider the following checklist of governance characteristics when assessing a firm.

Background of Board Members

- Are the board members mostly insiders?

- Do the board members have the proper background to oversee the firm's managers?

- Are the board members also serving on the boards of many other firms?

- What is the compensation structure of the board members?

  It is difficult for board members to be effective monitors of a firm if they are insiders, or if they have no background in the industry, or if they are serving on the boards of many other firms. In general, board members are more likely to be focused on maximizing the long-term value of the firm if their compensation structure provides them with stock in the firm that they must hold for a long period.

- How much work is involved in being on the board?

If all that board members have to do is simply show up at a board meeting every few months, then the board is not playing a significant role in overseeing management. There should be ongoing communication between top management and the board about the direction of the firm's business and about major policy issues.

- Do board members have access to the firm's managers?

If board members are unable to communicate with managers and are limited to discussions with the CEO, they will not be capable of proper monitoring.

Disclosure

- Is there a system in place by which the firm can periodically disclose its performance and financial condition?

The financial disclosure in the reports and documents filed with the Securities and Exchange Commission (SEC) should be complete, accurate, and transparent for investors. Employees should be encouraged to inform senior management if any reported information is incomplete or inaccurate.

Background of the Audit Committee

- Is the job description for the firm's audit committee members clear?
- Do the members of the audit committee have the ability to ensure that an independent audit will occur? Are they required to have specific credentials to certify that they have the ability that is required for the position?
- Do the members of the audit committee have the ability to interpret and respond to the auditors' concerns?
- Does the audit committee have easy access to the internal audit department of the firm?
- Is the audit committee required to provide a report of the work performed by the auditor to the board of directors?

Ethics Policy

- Does the firm have an ethics policy?
- Does the firm encourage directors, officers, and employees to report transactions that might be construed as a conflict of interest?
- Does the firm have guidelines regarding gifts from suppliers or other business relationships?

- Does the firm have guidelines about contributions that can prevent conflicts of interest?

- Does the firm have guidelines about loans to officers or directors?

- Does the firm have guidelines requiring consultants to be unrelated to officers or board members?

- Does the firm have guidelines that specify the maximum fees that may be paid to business consultants?

- Does the firm have guidelines regarding disciplinary action when one of its senior managers, board members, or other employees engages in unethical activities?

Insider Trading

- Does the firm have a policy on insider trading or a system for complying with rules that prevent insider trading?

- Does the firm define the types of inside information that could be construed as material, so that its directors, officers, and employees can recognize situations in which they should not be trading the firm's stock?

- Does the firm have guidelines regarding disciplinary action in response to illegal insider trading by its directors, senior managers, or employees?

VALUATION

By asking these common-sense questions about a business, you may be able to detect obvious problems so that you can eliminate a firm with these problems from your list of possible stocks to purchase. Conversely, if a firm is attractive based on the underlying business, the next step is to determine whether the price of the firm's stock already reflects the value of that business. There are many good businesses that would not be good investments because their stocks are priced too high.

A firm with good corporate governance is not automatically a wise investment. Some firms have a proper structure for reporting their performance, for serving customers, and for serving shareholders, but are overvalued. Their stock price is not warranted by the firm's business model and the potential cash flows that it can generate. Thus, a check on corporate governance may be a necessary first screen when selecting stocks, but it is not an indicator of undervalued stocks.

Valuation is difficult because it requires you to assign a dollar value based on limited subjective information that is subject to much uncertainty. Yet, you may at least be able to recognize when a stock's prevailing price is excessive given the information that you have.

For example, assume the following information:

- Your subjective judgment of a firm's management is that it is no better than the norm for the industry.

- The firm is just as exposed to industry and economic conditions as most other firms in the industry.

- The firm's debt ratio and its level of fixed costs are higher than the norm.

- The firm's price is a relatively high multiple of its expected earnings.

Given this information, you should not invest in this firm's stock. Without deriving a precise valuation of the stock, you were able to determine that the stock is priced relatively high compared to that of some other firms in the same industry, and that the stock's price is not justified by the firm's general business characteristics. In other words, if you really wanted to capitalize on favorable expectations about the prospects for that industry, you would probably invest in some other firm in the industry.

Some investors prefer a more precise method of valuation, so that they can directly compare their valuation to the prevailing market price of a stock. However, such a valuation must either convert subjective information into a formula or ignore the information. One compromise is to apply a quantitative model based on expected earnings or other objective (but possibly manipulated) data and to complement the analysis with a subjective assessment of the firm. In this case, the decision to invest in a stock would require both a valuation that is lower than the prevailing price and a favorable subjective assessment of the firm. When a firm has unfavorable characteristics, investors tend to use various methods for discounting the valuation, all of which are subject to error. For example, they may discount a firm's valuation by 5 percent because of the likelihood that new competitors will enter the industry in the next few months. These efforts to quantify subjective information allow investors to derive a specific valuation of the firm's stock, but they essentially create a decision model that is even more arbitrary than just using common sense to develop a subjective assessment of the firm.

21

USE A LONG-TERM PERSPECTIVE

I F YOU LOOK BEYOND THE RECENT EARNINGS NUMBERS and focus on characteristics that will shape the firm's future, you need to use a long-term perspective. That is, firms that are likely to perform well in the long term will not necessarily perform well this quarter, next quarter, or this year. When firms plan for the long run, they may have to sacrifice short-term earnings. That is, they may incur more expenses now and develop some projects slowly, resulting in slower revenue growth. Notice that these characteristics are the exact opposite of the strategies that some firms use to inflate their earnings. Recall that some firms attempt to report normal expenses as one-time expenses in order to make their earnings look better today. Investors will ultimately realize that these firms always have nonrecurring expenses. That is, their nonrecurring expenses keep recurring.

Unfortunately, managers of firms do not focus on the long run because they are attempting to appease investors who are focused on the short run. Institutional investors are given incentives and bonuses based on how they perform in the short term. They recognize that they may not be employed by their institutions in the long run, and the institutions recognize this as well. Thus, they focus on investments that they hope will pay off in the near future. Given this mindset by institutional investors, managers are discouraged from using a long-term perspective because they may be punished (by a lower stock price) for not focusing on the short run. Some corporate managers are given bonuses based on short-term performance, which is an additional reason why they are discouraged from using a long-term perspective.

SHIFTING THE FOCUS TO DEVELOPMENT

Nevertheless, there are some firms that are making a concerted effort to focus on the long-run perspective. One indicator is a firm whose reports focus on plans for the future development of its business. Firms that have a cohesive plan for growing their business tend to perform better than firms that simply acquire other companies (whether related to their prevailing business or not) as a means of achieving quick growth.

Another possible indicator of a long-term rather than a short-term perspective is that the firm does not provide continual earnings guidance (provide continual updates on what the reported earnings will be for the quarter). Coca-Cola, McDonald's, AT&T, and PepsiCo have recently discontinued their earnings guidance, and other firms are likely to follow their lead. Analysts tend to rely heavily on earnings guidance, because they serve many investors who use a short-term perspective. When a firm discontinues guidance, it may be signaling to analysts and other investors that it does not plan to devote so much effort to making sure that it meets this quarter's earnings expectations. Instead, it intends to focus on broader long-term issues that should take precedence over satisfying analysts in the current quarter.

Of course, it is possible that a firm will discontinue its earnings guidance but have no focus on long-term planning. Discontinued earnings guidance is a hint that the firm is shifting to a long-term perspective, but it should be complemented with other evidence that the firm is focused on a rational strategic plan for improving market share, efficiency, and the growth of its product line.

THE ROLE OF INVESTOR RELATIONS

Firms that use a long-term perspective will not please all investors, but they may be attractive to those investors who recognize the limitations and risks of trading on the basis of the latest earnings reports or rumors. It is easier to use deceptive accounting in the short run than to be deceptive about a general plan for the business. A firm's business plan is more transparent if it is articulated properly, so that the firm can be held accountable (by investors' dumping the shares) if it does not follow through on its plan. Given the transparency of a detailed business plan, managers of a firm are likely to follow through to make the plan happen. By using proper investor relations, firms can establish their credibility over time. After communicating their long-term plans, they can periodically document how their changes in operations are in line with their long-term plans.

Investors agree that a firm's value is dependent on its future cash flows, but some investors rely mostly on the latest earnings figures to derive a value, without seriously considering the firm's long-term prospects. Those investors who assess a firm's long-term prospects can incorporate that assessment when they estimate the firm's future cash flows and value the firm's stock. The process still requires some subjective judgment, but incorporating subjective judgment into a valuation is better than ignoring the information completely.

22

DON'T TRUST
ANYONE

T HE INFORMATION provided up to this point leads to four rules of investing that can provide a defense against deceptive accounting and unethical behavior in financial markets.

RULE 1: BE SUSPICIOUS OF A FIRM'S MANAGEMENT

There are two common mistakes that you can make when you are considering stocks to purchase: (1) being overly suspicious of a firm's management, which causes you to miss out on a feasible investment, or (2) being too naïve about a firm's management, which causes you to invest in a weak stock. It is better to err on the side of suspicion. There are thousands of stocks available, so there is no reason to invest in a stock unless you feel confident that the firm's management is not only efficient but also ethical.

Be alert for possible unethical behavior that can adversely affect the stock price. The recent accounting scandals provide numerous valuable lessons. Don't trust anyone when making investment decisions, including the firm's executives, its board members, and its auditors. The scandals do not mean that all stocks are overvalued, but they do mean that investors must be very cautious when selecting stocks. Investing in stocks can be sensible even for conservative investors, assuming that they invest within their information boundaries. If you want to gamble your money by undertaking risky strategies within the stock market, at least recognize the risk involved.

While the accounting scandals may ultimately result in greater regulation and enforcement, investors cannot assume that regulations will prevent other scandals in the future. While there are many reputable executives, board members, and auditors in the business world, it is difficult to distinguish those who are reputable from those who are not.

Even if there is more monitoring to ensure that the accounting is within the guidelines, the accounting rules still allow substantial flexibility. Consequently, some firms will still create misleading financial statements. In addition, there are still conflicts of interest that encourage a firm's executives, accountants, directors, and independent auditors to create or allow misleading financial statements. The most obvious example of this is when a firm uses accounting that is misleading, although it is within the rules, simply because other firms in the industry use the same type of accounting. This form of deceptive accounting will continue until the accounting standards are narrowed in a way that forces each firm to be more honest. As it stands, some firms feel forced to exaggerate their numbers within the rules just to keep up with the accounting used by their competitors.

There will still be firms that will try to inflate their stock's value, at least for a temporary period. There will still be executives who try to sell their shares while the stock is overvalued. There will still be analysts who rate stocks highly because of conflicts of interest. There will still be auditors who sign off on financial statements that are technically within the accounting guidelines, but are misleading to investors. There will still be board members who are unable to detect fraud by executives or auditors, or who are unwilling to report it. There will still be investors who will be adversely affected by all these actions.

Also recognize that even if a firm's managers are ethical, they may not necessarily be competent. In a fiercely competitive business world, many business ideas will fail. Even some firms with good business ideas struggle because they do not implement their business ideas efficiently. Their high cost of producing their products or services is essentially passed on to the shareholders.

RULE 2: BE SUSPICIOUS OF YOUR ABILITY TO VALUE STOCKS

The recent high-profile accounting fraud cases have made investors more aware that the financial statements reported by firms may be misleading. Some investors have taken the initiative in learning more about detecting accounting fraud. While such an education can be beneficial, it will not necessarily be sufficient for detecting accounting fraud. To illustrate, consider some of the examples of accounting fraud provided in this book. One of the most obvious examples is inflating operating earnings by counting some operating expenses as nonrecurring expenses. Yet, even if investors are trained to watch for this type of fraud, they will not have sufficient information to know whether the firm is committing it. Many firms do incur nonrecurring expenses, and should report these expenses in this manner. It is difficult for investors to identify the firms that have shifted some of their operating expenses over to nonrecurring expenses. In fact, investors are not likely to detect accounting fraud at firms other than those that blatantly abuse the accounting standards.

Regardless of how much accounting, finance, and math you know, stock price movements are difficult to anticipate. In some cases, your valuation method may be more precise than the methods used by other investors, but it is the entire set of investors that drives the demand for and supply of a stock, and therefore its price.

It is unrealistic to think that you can completely understand the value, risk, or the credibility of a firm just because you study all of its financial statements, even if you understand accounting. However, an assessment of financial statements may at least help you screen out the stocks of firms whose financial statements are confusing.

One lesson of the accounting scandals is that we should not make investments that we do not understand. Even if accounting laws are clarified, most of us still will not understand what we are investing in. The varied interpretations of accounting rules will still lead to disagreement among investors regarding the value of stocks. Given our limited valuation abilities, there will still be stocks that are undervalued and stocks that are overvalued.

If you decide to invest in individual stocks, consider buying the stocks of firms whose operations and financial condition are clearly explained in financial statements and reports. Then, once you screen your list of stocks and identify those with more transparent operations, you can attempt to conduct your own valuations in the search of stocks that are undervalued, or at least are not overvalued.

Fear and greed explain some investment behavior and managerial behavior. However, more mistakes occur because of greed. When investors are driven by greed, they are more likely to invest in firms that are managed by executives who are driven by greed. The executives have the upper hand, as they know more about their firms than investors do. Therefore, fear is an admirable trait for investors. It acknowledges the possibility of greed on the part of executives, board members, and auditors, and it reduces the possibility of being overly exposed to a stock that could experience an abrupt decline in its price.

RULE 3: BE SUSPICIOUS OF INVESTMENT ADVICE

Just as you have limitations when making investment decisions, so do investment advisers. Research has shown that, in general, professional portfolio managers have not outperformed stock market indexes. In addition, analyst ratings have not been accurate predictors of stock price movements. This was well documented in the 2001–2002 period, when most stocks fell substantially while being rated favorably by analysts.

Just because "experts" in the stock market or many of a company's employees invest in a stock does not guarantee that the firm's accounting can be trusted. Many institutional investors had very large investments in Enron stock up to the day the company went bankrupt. Many employees of Enron also had confidence in Enron stock, and lost most of their retirement funds because their pension was concentrated in that stock. If a firm's executives want to disguise the firm's financial condition, they can probably achieve their goal within current accounting guidelines.

RULE 4: LIMIT YOUR TRUST IN ANY PARTICULAR STOCK

If you buy individual stocks, you should buy a sufficient number so that you are well diversified. Some research suggests that you need at least 12 or 15 stocks to be well diversified. However, it is dangerous to generalize, since the effects of diversification are dependent on the mix of stocks that you consider. For example, if you purchase 100 technology stocks, you are not well diversified because a decline in the technology sector will cause major damage to your stock portfolio.

Since stock prices can change in an unpredictable manner, your stock portfolio is at risk. If you recognize your limitations, you can establish a diversified asset allocation (among different types of securities) that is less vulnerable to unanticipated swings in stock prices. Do not place too much trust in any one stock. Limit the amount of funds that you can lose as a result of possible deceptive accounting or unethical managerial behavior by individuals employed by a firm.

You may be astute enough or lucky enough to avoid being cheated by executives, accountants, board members, or auditors. But if you prefer to reduce your exposure to the possibility of being cheated, you should consider investing in a broadly diversified stock portfolio. You can easily achieve broad diversification by investing in mutual funds or exchange-traded funds, which are discussed in subsequent chapters. This strategy will not necessarily make you rich, but it may prevent you from becoming poor. Diversification reduces your exposure to accounting scandals or other risks that could suddenly cause a sharp decline in your portfolio.

C H A P T E R

23

INVEST IN
MUTUAL FUNDS

THE ACCOUNTING scandals document how investors are subject
to potential losses as a result of deceptive accounting. You can
avoid heavy exposure to the next Enron or WorldCom by diversifying your stock portfolio. Mutual funds offer an easy and
low-cost method of diversifying, even if you have only a small
amount of funds to invest.

BACKGROUND ON STOCK MUTUAL FUNDS

Stock mutual funds specialize in investing in stock portfolios for individual
investors. They sell shares to individuals and invest the proceeds in stocks.
Each mutual fund employs portfolio managers who decide how to invest
the proceeds. These managers manage the stock portfolio, so that the individual investors do not have to select stocks themselves.

The minimum investment in a stock mutual fund is usually between $500 and $3000, depending on the fund. An investment of $3000 is not even large enough to invest in 100 shares of a single stock whose share price exceeds $30. By investing in a mutual fund, investors can become partial owners of a broadly diversified portfolio with only a small initial investment. The value of the shares changes in accordance with the value of the underlying stocks in the mutual fund's portfolio.

Some mutual funds are managed by commercial banks or investment banks. Many investment companies or other financial institutions manage a "family," or group, of separately managed mutual funds. Each mutual fund has its own investment objective. You can diversify your investments further by investing in various mutual funds within a given family.

When shareholders invest in a mutual fund, they purchase shares at a price equal to the fund's net asset value (NAV) per share. The NAV of a mutual fund is the difference between the market value of the fund's assets and its liabilities. The NAV per share is the NAV divided by the number of shares outstanding. At the end of each day, the market value of all investments held by the mutual fund is estimated. Dividend income is included on that day if particular stocks within the fund paid dividends on that day. Next, mailing, marketing, or other expenses charged to the fund or any dividends distributed to the fund's shareholders (investors) are deducted from the market value of the assets. The NAV changes over time in response to the market valuations of the stocks. The NAV per share of mutual funds is disclosed daily in the *Wall Street Journal* and many other financial newspapers, and also on many web sites.

The return to investors from investing in a mutual fund is primarily based on the net asset value per share at the time the shares are sold versus the NAV when they were purchased. This gain is taxed at the ordinary income tax rate when investors redeem their shares.

If the mutual fund invests in stocks that appreciate substantially over time, the net asset value per share should rise substantially, thereby generating large capital gains for shareholders. If the holding period of the investment is 1 year or less, the capital gain earned by the fund and distributed to shareholders is taxed as ordinary income. If the holding period is more than 1 year, the capital gain distributed to shareholders is taxed at capital gains tax rates. Some mutual funds also generate dividend income as a result of investing in dividend-paying stocks.

Open-End versus Closed-End Funds

Funds are classified as either open-end or closed-end. Open-end mutual funds sell shares to investors at any time, and stand ready to repurchase those shares whenever investors wish to sell them. Open-end mutual funds can either use cash or sell some of their investments to cover redemptions by investors.

A closed-end fund does not continuously sell shares to investors, nor does it accommodate redemptions. After a closed-end fund is created, its shares are purchased and sold on a stock exchange. The market price per share of a closed-end fund tends to move with the NAV of the fund. However, the fund's market price per share sometimes reflects a premium or a discount relative to the fund's NAV per share. For example, a closed-end fund could experience a slight decline in its price even though its NAV per share increased over a particular period.

Comparison of Load and No-Load Funds

Some open-end mutual funds sell shares directly to investors and do not charge a fee. They are referred to as no-load funds. Other open-end mutual funds charge a fee (or load) and are referred to as load mutual funds. The fee typically ranges from 1 to 8 percent of the initial investment. Investors who know the type of mutual fund that they want to invest in can avoid those fees by investing in no-load funds. The fee on load funds is commonly used to compensate the broker who advised the investor to invest in the load funds. Brokers do not normally guide an investor toward no-load funds, because there is no fee incentive to do so. If you wish to invest in no-load funds, you can easily access much information by visiting their web sites. Use a search term such as *no-load fund* in any search engine to access various related web sites.

By avoiding fees at the time of your investment, you can enhance your return.

Assume that you have the choice of investing in either a no-load fund or a fund that focuses on similar stocks, but has an 8 percent load. If the no-load fund's NAV per share rises by 10 percent, you receive all of that return. Conversely, if the load fund appreciates by 10 percent, most of that appreciation is offset by the fee you incurred.

While the load fund's portfolio generated a 10 percent return, you earned only a small return from investing in that fund, because you were charged a substantial load fee. Thus, the portfolio earned slightly more than the fee you were charged to buy the fund.

Load funds would be justified in charging fees if they outperformed no-load funds that have a similar investment objective by an amount that offsets the fee. However, there is no evidence to suggest that the portfolio managers of load funds are better stock pickers than the portfolio managers of no-load funds. If the portfolio management of the two types of funds is similar for a particular type of investment objective, the no-load funds should provide higher returns to shareholders.

If you invest money for a long period of time, the initial fee that you pay when investing in a load fund will not have such a pronounced effect on your long-term return. However, you should not hold a mutual fund for a long period of time just to reduce the effect of the load fee.

Expense Ratios

Mutual funds incur expenses as a result of managing a portfolio of securities, providing information to prospective shareholders, and accommodating redemption requests by shareholders. For a given type of investment objective, some mutual funds have higher expenses than others. Prospective shareholders should compare the expense of different mutual funds for a particular investment objective, since the expenses may be the most important factor causing one mutual fund to outperform another. The mutual fund that has the lowest expenses does not always outperform all others with the same investment objective. However, some mutual funds are more efficient than others, and therefore maintain their expenses at a lower level.

A common way to compare expenses across mutual funds is by using the expense ratio, which measures the annual expenses per share divided by the fund's net asset value per share. This ratio controls for the size of the fund, and therefore provides a level playing field for comparing the expenses of a large fund to those of a small fund. If a mutual fund has an expense ratio of 2 percent, its shareholders pay annual expenses equal to 2 percent of the fund's value. This is a relatively large expense ratio, considering that some funds have an expense ratio of less than 1 percent.

TYPES OF STOCK MUTUAL FUNDS

The first step in selecting a mutual fund is to determine your investment objective. There are many types of funds, so you should select the type of fund that fits your needs. Growth funds tend to focus on the stocks of firms that should experience relatively high growth. Capital appreciation funds invest in the stocks of firms that should experience very high growth. These firms tend to be relatively young and therefore may exhibit a high level of risk.

Income mutual funds invest in firms that pay a high level of dividends. These firms are more mature and have fewer growth opportunities, and therefore are able to distribute a higher percentage of their earnings as dividends. These firms tend to be more stable but are less likely to experience very high returns. Balanced growth and income funds include a combination of growth stocks and stocks that pay high dividends. They serve investors who want more income than they get from growth stocks, but more potential for high returns than income stocks provide. Sector funds invest in stocks that are within a particular industry or sector, and are attractive to investors who anticipate high performance from a particular sector.

Index funds are mutual funds that attempt to mirror the movements of specific stock indexes. These funds enable investors to earn returns similar to the change in the index. A wide variety of stock indexes are replicated by index funds, some including only large stocks, only mid-cap stocks, only small stocks, or even only stocks of a particular foreign country. Index funds are attractive because their passive portfolio management allows for very low expense ratios. That is, the expenses involved in trying to mimic an existing index are significantly lower than the expenses associated with trying to beat the performance of an index. Many index funds have expense ratios that are at least 1 percentage point less than actively managed mutual funds with a similar investment objective. This means that the actively managed funds would have to achieve a portfolio return of at least 1 percentage point more than index funds with the same investment objective in order to offset their higher expenses. If you decide to invest in an index fund because of its low expense ratio, make sure you check its expense ratio first. Some index funds have relatively high expense ratios. You should be able to find an index mutual fund that both serves your investment objective and has a low expense ratio.

International mutual funds invest in stocks issued by firms that are based outside of the United States. Some of these funds invest only within a single country, while others spread their investments across a specific region. International mutual funds are attractive to investors who want to invest in foreign stocks and rely on professionals to make the investment decisions. If investors simply want to invest in a portfolio that mimics a foreign stock index, they may prefer to invest in index funds representing that index rather than in an actively managed portfolio. The expenses associated with actively managing an international stock fund tend to be high, but an index fund representing a foreign stock index should have a lower expense ratio.

Dividends and capital gains earned by the mutual fund may be distributed to you in the form of a check or as additional shares of the fund. Regardless of the form of the distribution, the dividends that you receive from a mutual fund are taxed at your marginal income tax rate.

It is more difficult to determine your capital gain when you have reinvested any distributions in the fund, because each distribution results in the purchase of more shares at the prevailing price on that day. Thus, the capital gain on the additional shares purchased at the time of the distribution is dependent on the price at which you purchased those shares. Many investors rely on the mutual fund to report capital gain after they redeem the shares.

All stock funds are exposed to stock market conditions, but the degree of exposure varies. An income fund is normally less sensitive to stock market conditions than a capital appreciation fund because the income fund contains more mature stocks. These stocks are not expected to perform as well as capital appreciation stocks during strong market conditions or as poorly during weak stock market conditions. International stock funds may be less sensitive to U.S. stock market conditions, but they are very sensitive to stock market conditions in the countries in which the fund has its investments.

REVIEWING A STOCK FUND'S PROSPECTUS

When you are considering an investment in a stock mutual fund, obtain a prospectus for that fund. You can typically order the prospectus by phone, and you may even be able to download it from a web site.

The prospectus discloses

- The investment objective of the fund, such as whether it focuses on growth stocks, dividend stocks, foreign stocks, or an index.

- The investment strategy (also called investment policy) summarizing the types of securities that are purchased by the mutual fund in order to achieve its objective.

- Recent performance, including the return on the fund over the last year, the last 3 years, and the last 5 years. When assessing a fund's recent performance, compare the fund to a benchmark index over the same period to control for general market conditions. If a fund generated a 15 percent return over a given period while a benchmark index generated a 25 percent return, the fund's performance is relatively weak. Many investors purchase in mutual funds that have performed well recently. However, you cannot assume that past performance of a mutual fund will continue in the future.

- Recent expenses, including the maximum load imposed on purchases of the fund's shares and the back-end load (if any) charged to investors who sell their shares back to the mutual fund. The fund's expenses are also disclosed, such as fees resulting from managing the fund's portfolio, distribution (12b-1) fees incurred when advertising the fund, and marketing costs that are paid to brokers who recommend the funds to investors.

- Frequency of dividend and capital gains distributions. Many funds distribute their dividends to their shareholders on a quarterly basis and distribute their capital gains once a year (usually in December).

- The minimum investment needed to invest in the fund.

- The process for investing in the fund.

BACKGROUND ON BOND MUTUAL FUNDS

Bond mutual funds sell shares to investors, and their portfolio managers invest the proceeds in bonds. Individuals can take part ownership in a well-diversified bond portfolio with an investment of $3000. Bond funds are commonly managed by the same investment companies that manage stock funds. Investors who invest in stock and bond funds within the same family can typically transfer money from one fund to another.

Bond funds also incur expenses for portfolio management, marketing, and other operations. However, the expenses of bond funds are less than those of stock funds because the management of a bond fund portfolio requires less resources.

Shares of open-end bond funds are sold directly to investors by the fund, and are repurchased when investors want to sell the shares. Shares of closed-end bond funds are purchased by investors on a stock exchange and are sold on that exchange.

Bond mutual funds receive interest income from their investments and allocate this income to their shareholders in the form of dividend distributions. They also generate capital gains when bonds in the fund's portfolio are sold at a higher price than the purchase price. These capital gains distributions are taxed at the long-term capital gains tax rate. Investors also receive a capital gain if they redeem shares in the bond mutual fund at a share price that exceeds the price they paid for the shares. If the shares are held for more than 1 year, they are subject to a long-term capital gain tax rate. If they are held for 1 year or less, they are subject to the ordinary income tax rate.

Bond fund performance is influenced by interest-rate movements because movements in the prices of bonds are inversely related to interest-rate movements. Therefore, the prices of bond funds are normally inversely related to interest rate movements. However, the sensitivity of bond funds to interest rates varies with the maturities of the bonds. Bonds with long-term maturities are more sensitive.

Types of Bond Mutual Funds

Investors select bond funds that satisfy their investment objectives. Shares of Treasury bond funds avoid default risk. Shares of funds that invest in bonds issued by other government agencies offer a slightly higher return and have a low degree of default risk. Corporate bond funds have various levels of potential return and risk. Some bond funds focus on the highest-quality bonds, while "high-yield" bond funds focus on low-quality (junk) bonds. The high-yield bond funds offer a higher expected return but also are exposed to more risk. Bond funds that focus on long-term maturities have more potential for a high return in the future if interest rates decline, but more potential risk of poor returns if interest rates rise.

Municipal bond funds invest in municipal bonds. The interest income on municipal bonds is exempt from federal taxes, and therefore is very appealing to investors in high tax brackets. Another option is international bond funds, which invest in bonds issued by governments or firms in foreign countries. The performance of these funds is affected by the change in the value of the currencies in which the bonds are denominated. That is, if the foreign currencies in which the bonds are denominated appreciate against the dollar, the value of the bonds (from a U.S. perspective) increases. Conversely, the depreciation of foreign currencies causes the value of foreign bonds to decline from a U.S. perspective.

For any type of bond funds, there are different maturity levels. For example, Treasury bond funds are commonly segmented into short-term, medium-term, and long-term funds. If several bonds maintained within a fund's portfolio default on payments, the bond fund will perform poorly. Past performance is not necessarily a good indicator of the bond fund's future performance because economic conditions change over time.

If you plan to invest in bond funds, you should determine the type of bond fund that fits the degree of default risk and interest-rate risk that you are willing to accept. You can avoid default risk by investing in Treasury bond funds, but you will still be exposed to interest-rate risk. You can minimize interest-rate risk by selecting a bond fund with shorter maturities. If you expect economic conditions to be favorable and you are willing to tolerate a high degree of default risk, you can invest in a high-yield bond fund. If you expect interest rates to decline, you can benefit from investing in a fund with long-term maturities.

Reviewing a Bond Fund's Prospectus

Before you invest in a bond mutual fund, review its prospectus. The prospectus of a bond fund provides information about the minimum investment required to purchase shares of the fund, the types of bonds that it purchases, the typical maturities of the bonds that it purchases, the fund's recent performance, and its fees and expenses, including its expense ratio.

REAL ESTATE INVESTMENT TRUSTS

A real estate investment trust (REIT) (pronounced "reet") is a closed-end fund that uses investors' money to invest in real estate properties or mortgages. A REIT is similar to other closed-end funds, except that its assets are real estate rather than stocks or bonds. Like other closed-end funds, REITs are listed on stock exchanges. REITs allow investors to invest in a diversified portfolio of real estate properties or mortgages managed by professionals with a small initial investment. While REITs are diversified, the values of the properties in a REIT investment portfolio are highly influenced by real estate conditions. Thus, if real estate conditions deteriorate, a REIT that is focused on properties is likely to perform poorly.

24

INVEST IN EXCHANGE-TRADED FUNDS

I NVESTORS WHO INVEST A HIGH PROPORTION OF THEIR FUNDS IN ONE OR A FEW STOCKS are exposed to potential losses as a result of deceptive accounting. They can reduce their exposure to the accounting of any individual stock by investing in a widely diversified portfolio of stocks representing a specific stock market, sector, or industry. Many investors prefer to target particular markets or industries rather than individual firms. For example, they may believe that the biotechnology sector will perform well in the future because of the potential innovations within that sector, but they will not necessarily know which biotech firms will perform the best. Alternatively, they may believe that the Japanese stock market will perform well because of recent economic reforms in Japan, but they will not necessarily know which Japanese stocks will perform the best.

MOTIVATION FOR INVESTING IN A STOCK INDEX

There are several advantages to investing in indexes. First, they represent a diversified portfolio, so their performance is not dependent on a single firm's operations. Second, since a single purchase of an index allows you to invest in a number of stocks, it is subject to smaller transaction costs than if you purchased several different stocks on your own. Third, indexes tend to perform just as well as or better than stock portfolios (such as some mutual funds) that are actively managed by professional portfolio managers. The results of such a comparison can vary over time, and some portfolio managers outperform indexes in any given period. However, on average, the indexes perform well in comparison to portfolio managers. Therefore, many investors may be more comfortable with a passive investment such as an index than with a portfolio that is actively managed.

CHARACTERISTICS OF ETFs

Exchange-traded funds (ETFs) are designed to mimic particular stock indexes and are traded on a stock exchange. They are similar to index mutual funds in that their share price adjusts over time in response to the change in the index level. In addition, they pay dividends in the form of additional shares to investors. Since they are intended to track an index, their portfolio management is relatively simple, resulting in lower management fees than mutual funds.

ETFs are unique because they can be traded throughout the day, unlike mutual funds. Closed-end funds are also traded throughout the day. However, closed-end funds are typically actively managed. In addition, the share prices of closed-end funds commonly differ from the value of the securities that are contained within the portfolio. Therefore, the share prices of closed-end funds can decline even when there is no decline in the value of the portfolio. Investors in closed-end funds are subject to the risk that the price of the shares will decline even if the prices of stocks within the fund do not decline. Unlike closed-end funds, the price of an ETF is normally similar to the value of its portfolio.

ETFs can also be purchased on margin, allowing investors to partially finance their investment with borrowed funds from a broker. Another advantage of ETFs is their tax advantage. If an index is revised, an ETF needs to be revised to mimic the revised index. When stocks held by an

ETF are sold, there is no tax effect on investors, as there would be with mutual funds. Investors are subject to capital gains taxes only when they sell their shares.

One disadvantage of ETFs compared to index mutual funds is that transaction costs are incurred every time an investor purchases shares because a broker is needed to purchase the shares. Conversely, investors can invest in a no-load index mutual fund periodically without incurring transactions costs because no broker is involved.

TYPES OF ETFs

There are many types of ETFs available for investors. Investors who want to invest in an index representing technology firms can invest in the Cubes (the trading symbol is QQQ), traded on the American Stock Exchange, which represent the Nasdaq 100 index. This index has a heavy concentration of technology firms, and its value tracks the general sentiment regarding the technology sector. Investors who anticipate rising stock values in the technology sector but do not know which stocks will perform the best may consider Cubes.

Another popular ETF is the Standard & Poor's Depository Receipt (also called Spider), which is intended to mimic the price movements of the S&P 500 index. Investors who anticipate that the large U.S. firms included in the S&P 500 index will perform well but do not necessarily know which stocks will perform the best should consider purchasing Spiders. Spiders are valued at one-tenth the S&P 500 value. When the S&P 500 is valued at $1600, a Spider is valued at $160. The appreciation of the share price is similar to the appreciation in the value of the S&P 500 index.

Diamonds track the Dow Jones Industrial Average (DJIA) and are valued at one one-hundredth of the DJIA value. The DJIA is a much narrower index than the S&P 500 because it includes only 30 stocks. There are also ETFs available for investors who wish to invest in indexes made up of smaller stocks. For example, Mid-Cap Spiders track the S&P 400 Mid-Cap Index.

Some ETFs track specific sectors or industries. For example, there are ETFs that mirror a basic materials index, a chemicals index, an energy index, a financial sector index, a health-care index, an Internet index, a real estate index, a technology index, a telecommunications index, and a utilities index. There are also ETFs that track the stock indexes of specific countries, such as Australia, Austria, Belgium, Brazil, Canada, France, Germany, Hong Kong, Italy, Japan, Malaysia, Mexico, Singapore, South Korea, Sweden, and Taiwan. These ETFs allow investors to invest in foreign stock markets at a relatively low cost. Since these ETFs are designed to simply mimic existing foreign stock indexes, they avoid the expenses that would be associated with attempting to actively manage stocks in foreign stock markets.

C H A P T E R

25

INVEST IN OTHER SECURITIES

I F YOU SENSE THAT INVESTORS ARE VALUING STOCKS HIGHER THAN WHAT IS APPROPRIATE given the reported financial condition of firms, consider investing in other securities. Some of the more popular types of securities are identified here. Some of these securities are subject to risk, including the risk of deceptive accounting by firms.

PREFERRED STOCK

Preferred stock is a form of equity stake in a corporation that usually does not allow for significant voting rights. Preferred shareholders have priority over common shareholders in terms of receiving dividend payments. Most preferred stock has a cumulative provision, which prevents dividends from being paid on common stock until all preferred stock dividends (both current and those previously omitted) have been paid. However, if the firm does not have sufficient earnings to pay the preferred stock dividends, it may omit the dividend without being forced into bankruptcy. While preferred stock is considered to be safer than common stock, its value can decline substantially if the firm performs poorly.

MONEY MARKET SECURITIES

Money market securities are debt securities that have a maturity of 1 year or less. Many money market securities are traded frequently in secondary markets, and therefore are very liquid; that is, they can easily be turned into cash. They are also considered to be liquid because of their short maturities, which means that they will be redeemed by the issuer in the near future. Money market securities commonly have a low expected return. However, they usually have a low level of risk, meaning that there is a low level of uncertainty surrounding the expected return.

Treasury Bills

Treasury bills (T-bills) are short-term debt securities issued by the U.S. Treasury to obtain short-term funds. The minimum par value (the amount received by investors at maturity) of T-bills is $1000, and they are issued in multiples of $1000 thereafter. The minimum level was reduced from $10,000 so that more individual investors would be able to invest in T-bills. T-bills are sold through auctions; 3- and 6-month T-bills are sold weekly, while 1-year T-bills are sold monthly. In the summer of 2001, the Treasury began to include 4-week Treasury bills in its weekly auction.

Investors can either hold the T-bills until maturity or sell them before maturity to other investors in the secondary market. This market is served by government securities dealers, who act as intermediaries to match up investors who want to sell Treasury bills before they reach maturity with investors who want to buy them.

T-bills are highly liquid. In general, investors prefer liquid securities because they know that they can easily sell them to obtain cash. Some investors are willing to accept the lower rate of return on Treasury securities because of the liquidity advantage.

T-bills are risk-free for investors in that they are backed by the federal government and thus are free of credit (default) risk. This is another desirable characteristic that explains why T-bills are attractive even if they offer a lower return than other types of securities. Investors purchase T-bills at a discount from their par value. When they hold T-bills until maturity, they earn a return that is based on the difference between the par value of the bills and the amount paid by investors. Investors who do not hold the T-bills until maturity earn a return that is based on the difference between the amount they received when they sell the T-bills and the amount they paid for them.

Money Market Funds

Money market funds pool money received from investors and use it to invest in money market securities. They also allow individuals who invest funds to write checks against the account, although there may be some restrictions applied. Money market funds typically invest in T-bills and in short-term debt securities issued by firms.

BONDS

Bonds are long-term debt obligations issued by corporations and government agencies to support their operations. They generate interest income for investors in the form of coupon payments every 6 months. Their maturities are typically between 10 and 30 years. Bearer bonds require the owner to send coupons to the issuer in order to receive interest payments. Registered bonds require the issuer to maintain records of who owns the bond and send interest payments to the owners. The issuer of a bond pays interest (or coupon) payments periodically (such as annually or semiannually) and the par value (principal) to investors at maturity.

The corporate bond market is facilitated by bond dealers who match up willing buyers and sellers. Corporate bonds can now be purchased online by individuals through various online bond brokerage web sites.

More than 2000 bonds issued by U.S. and foreign firms are listed on the New York Stock Exchange (NYSE). Some bonds are sold on the American Stock Exchange, and others are not listed on any exchange, but are simply sold over the counter (through a telecommunications network). Even the bonds that are listed on a stock exchange are traded through a telecommunications network.

Treasury Bonds

The U.S. Treasury commonly issues Treasury bonds to finance the expenditures of the federal government. The minimum denomination for Treasury bonds is $1000. The government also issues Treasury notes, which have maturities of less than 10 years, as compared with 10 years or more for bonds.

Firms and individuals are common investors in Treasury bonds. If investors decide not to hold Treasury bonds and notes until maturity, they can easily sell them in the secondary market. Bond dealers serve the secondary market by matching up buyers and sellers of Treasury bonds. The trading of bonds in the secondary market is conducted through a telecommunications network. Individual investors can purchase Treasury bonds online through a web site established by the Treasury.

The interest received by investors holding Treasury bonds is taxed by the federal government as ordinary income, but is exempt from any state and local taxes.

Federal Agency Bonds

Federal agency bonds are bonds issued by federal agencies. One of the primary roles of the federal agencies that issue bonds is to invest in mortgages, thus supplying funds to individuals who are purchasing homes. The Government National Mortgage Association (Ginnie Mae) issues bonds and uses the proceeds to purchase mortgages that are insured by the Federal Housing Administration (FHA) and by the Veterans Administration (VA). The Federal Home Loan Mortgage Association (called Freddie Mac) issues bonds and uses the proceeds to purchase conventional mortgages. The Federal National Mortgage Association (Fannie Mae) is a federally chartered corporation that issues bonds and uses the proceeds to purchase residential mortgages.

Municipal Bonds

Municipal bonds are issued by state and local governments to support a variety of public projects. They can be classified as either general obligation bonds or revenue bonds. General obligation bonds are backed by the municipal government's ability to tax. In contrast, payments on revenue bonds must be generated from the revenues of the project (such as a tollway) that was supported by the issuance of the bonds. The minimum denomination of municipal bonds is typically $5000. General obligation and revenue bonds pay interest on a semiannual basis. The interest income provided by municipal bonds is normally exempt from federal taxes, and is sometimes exempt from state and local taxes.

The most common purchasers of municipal bonds are financial institutions and individuals. There is a secondary market, but many municipal bonds have limited secondary market activity. Municipal bond dealers serve the secondary market by matching up investors who want to buy or sell municipal bonds.

Corporate Bonds

Corporate bonds are long-term debt securities issued by corporations. They have a minimum denomination of $1000, and they pay interest on a semi-annual basis. The typical maturity of corporate bonds is between 10 and 30 years, but some bonds have longer terms. There is a secondary market for corporate bonds, but many bonds have limited activity.

Indenture

The obligations undertaken by a corporation that is issuing bonds are summarized in the indenture, which is a legal document specifying the rights and obligations of both the issuing firm and the bondholders. Bond indentures frequently include a sinking-fund provision, which forces the firm to retire a certain amount of the bond issue each year. They also include protective covenants, which restrict the issuing firm from taking certain actions that would increase the risk of default on the bonds. For example, protective covenants may be used to limit the amount of dividends that the firm can pay to its shareholders. The indenture may also include a call provision, allowing the firm to buy back the bonds before they mature. This provision is valuable to the issuing firm because it can retire bonds with high interest rates when market interest rates decline and conduct a new bond offering at the prevailing lower interest rates. Since a call provision may require bondholders to redeem their bonds sooner than planned, corporate bonds that contain a call provision must offer slightly higher yields than bonds without a call provision.

The indenture also specifies whether the bonds are secured by collateral and the type of collateral. Many bonds use a mortgage on property (land and buildings) as collateral. A first mortgage bond has first claim on the specified assets. A chattel mortgage bond is secured by personal property. There are also corporate bonds that are not backed by collateral, called debentures. Corporations that do not provide collateral will have to pay a higher return on bonds than they would if they had backed the bonds with collateral.

The indenture will also specify whether the bonds are convertible into shares of the issuing firm's stock. Convertible bonds are long-term debt securities that are convertible into a specified number of shares of the issuing firm's common stock. These bonds pay a lower interest rate than other bonds with similar features that are not convertible, but they have the potential to provide a higher return if the issuing firm's stock performs well.

Return

Investors who invest in a bond when it is issued and hold it until maturity will earn the stated yield to maturity. However, investors who do not want to hold a bond to maturity can sell the bond in the secondary market. The return they will receive on their investment is determined by the coupon payments received plus the difference between the selling price and the purchase price of the bond.

Default Risk

A bond's price could decline to zero if the issuer were to default on the debt. Investors who are holding the bond will not be able to either sell it or redeem it with the issuer. Just as investors must watch out for deceptive accounting when they invest in stocks, they must also watch out for it when they invest in corporate bonds. Investors can reduce their exposure to the possibility of deceptive accounting by investing in a bond mutual fund rather than investing in a single corporate bond. Since the price at which a bond may be sold in the secondary market is uncertain, the return to be earned on even bonds free from default risk that are not held until maturity is uncertain.

Credit Ratings

Since corporate bonds are subject to possible default by the issuers, investors assess the creditworthiness of the companies issuing corporate bonds before they buy these bonds. They may rely on credit rating agencies rather than attempt to assess the risk of corporate bonds themselves. Credit rating agencies assign quality ratings to corporate bonds based on their assessment of the issuer's default risk. Each rating agency has its own method for assessing a firm's creditworthiness. However, these agencies focus on the types of characteristics that would affect a firm's ability to repay its debt, such as its prevailing level of debt and its revenue.

Rating agencies are not always able to detect when a firm's financial condition is weak. Some firms have used deceptive accounting that hid their financial problems. Consequently, investors in bonds are exposed to possible losses as a result of deceptive accounting, just as investors in stocks are.

A P P E N D I X

INVESTING IN INDIVIDUAL STOCKS

While stocks are an attractive investment for even conservative investors, stock mutual funds or exchange-traded funds are more effective for most investors than the purchase of individual stocks. Nevertheless, many investors still prefer to invest in individual stocks. For this reason, general information is provided here.

STOCK QUOTATIONS

Stock quotations summarize the results of trading activity on stock exchanges. They are given in financial newspapers such as the *Wall Street Journal, Barron's,* and *Investor's Business Daily,* and in some local newspapers. Each newspaper uses its own format for reporting the quotations, but most newspapers disclose the same information. Although the format varies among newspapers, most quotations provide the following information for stocks traded on the New York Stock Exchange (NYSE), American Stock Exchange (AMEX), and Nasdaq:

143

- Symbol used to identify the firm (for example, Cisco Systems is CSCO)
- Closing stock price per share
- Change in the stock price per share from the previous day
- Range of the stock's price over the last year
- Annual dividends paid on the stock
- Dividend yield, which represents the annual dividends divided by the prevailing stock price
- Price/earnings ratio, which is the stock's price per share divided by the firm's earnings per share for the last year
- Volume of shares traded during the previous day

STOCK INDEX QUOTATIONS

In addition to stock quotations, stock index quotations are also given in many newspapers. These quotations summarize the stock market performance of a specific set of stocks. They represent the performance of the overall market or of a particular subset of the market.

Dow Jones Industrial Average

The Dow Jones Industrial Average (DJIA) is a price-weighted average of the stock prices of 30 large U.S. firms, such as Coca-Cola, Exxon, General Motors, and IBM. Since this index is based on only 30 large stocks, it is used to assess the general market conditions for large stocks. It is not a useful indicator of small-stock performance.

Standard & Poor's 500

The Standard & Poor's (S&P) 500 index is a value-weighted index of the stock prices of 500 large U.S. firms. It includes a much larger number of firms than the DJIA. It is commonly used by investors as a benchmark for assessing the performance of their investments. For example, investors may determine the return on their stocks during a recent period and compare it to the return on the S&P 500 index.

New York Stock Exchange Indexes

There are stock indexes that track the stocks traded on the NYSE. The Composite Index is the average of all the stocks traded on the NYSE. Since there are more than 3000 stocks traded on the NYSE, this index is a very broad measure of stock market conditions. It can be used to assess how stocks in general have performed during a specific period.

Sector Indexes

Some investors may prefer to focus on a particular sector rather than on the entire stock market. For this reason, the NYSE, AMEX, and Nasdaq offer various indexes that cover subsets of stocks in a particular sector that trade on that exchange. For example, the NYSE offers quotations for the industrial, transportation, utility, and financial stock indexes. Each index is a measure of the performance of the firms of the type described by that index whose stocks are traded on the NYSE. Different sectors can experience quite different performance levels in a particular period, so a general assessment of the market conditions cannot be automatically applied to every sector. Investors who have invested in a utility company may compare the performance of their investment to a utility index. If the investors' performance is weak, but is not as weak as that of the sector in general, they realize that their weak performance is due to unfavorable conditions in that sector. Alternatively, if their investment performance is weak while the utility index increased substantially, their weak performance can be attributed to the performance of the specific firm in which they invested. Similarly, investors who invested in a manufacturing company may compare their investment performance to the industrial index. The indexes serve as useful benchmarks because they can be used to determine how the sector has performed.

If you decide to purchase individual stocks or stock indexes, you must determine

- The type of order
- How to execute your order
- Whether to buy on margin
- Whether to take a short position

You can limit your risk and your expenses if you understand the different types of orders, the different types of brokerage firms, and the risks associated with margin trading and short sales.

SELECTING THE TYPE OF ORDER

When engaging in stock transactions, investors may use market orders or limit orders. Market orders are executed at the prevailing market price, while limit orders are executed based on the limit price specified.

For example, suppose you notice that a stock that you wish to purchase is presently quoted at $30 per share. If you submit a market order for the stock, the order will definitely be executed, but the price that you pay for the stock could exceed $30 if the market price increased before the trade was executed. Alternatively, you could submit a limit order, in which you state that you will pay only up to a specified amount for the stock. However, if the stock is higher than your specified limit, the transaction will not be executed. A limit order can be submitted just for the day or for a longer period of time. The advantage of a limit order is that you can ensure that your order will not be executed at a price that exceeds the price you wish to pay.

EXECUTING YOUR ORDER

When they purchase stocks, investors rely on brokers and specialists to execute the order. The roles of brokers and specialists are described here.

Brokers

Traditionally, an investor who wants to buy or sell stock contacts her or his broker and requests a specific transaction. The broker then communicates the information to a floor broker on the exchange where the stock is traded. On stock exchanges where there is a trading floor, such as the New York Stock Exchange, floor brokers execute the transactions transmitted to the exchange. If they are attempting to buy stock for a customer, they communicate their request to other floor brokers who are trying to sell the same stock for their customers. When the floor brokers agree on a price, the transaction is executed and recorded. The floor broker then contacts the customer's broker, who calls the customer to confirm the transaction.

In recent years, the online brokerage system has become popular. Most of the traditional brokerage firms now have an online service for investors who prefer to request their orders online and have 24-hour access to their accounts.

Discount brokerage firms execute transactions, but do not provide advice. Full-service brokerage firms not only execute transactions, but also provide advice regarding which stocks to buy or sell. Full-service brokers typically charge higher transaction fees than discount brokers because of the extra services they offer. Investors should consider fees when choosing a brokerage firm and estimating their return on an investment. The potential savings is especially large with larger orders. Some discount brokers charge a small fixed amount, such as $25, whether the order is for 100 shares or 900 shares. Conversely, some full-service brokers charge a commission that is a percentage of the amount of the order, so the commission increases with the size of the order. Commissions can vary among discount and full-service brokers, so conduct your own analysis before you decide on a discount or full-service broker. There is no convincing evidence that advice from full-service brokers leads to higher returns. If you decide to use a full-service broker because you are uncomfortable selecting stocks, you may want to consider investing your money in one or more mutual funds (discussed later) that have low fees and are well diversified.

Role of Specialists and Market Makers

Specialists can also execute the trades desired by investors. Their profit is the difference between the ask price at which they sell a stock and the bid price at which they would be willing to buy it. That is, if they buy a particular stock from one customer at their bid price of $22.30 and then sell the stock to another customer at their ask price of $22.40, they earn the $0.10 difference (or "spread") on each share of stock traded in this transaction.

Specialists hold inventories of the stocks that they trade. Thus, they can execute a buy order by selling some of the stock that they own rather than matching up the buy order with a sell order from another customer. They can execute a sell order by buying the stock themselves rather than matching up the sell order with a buy order by another customer. Thus, they can provide liquidity to the market.

The Nasdaq market does not have a trading floor or specialists. Instead, the market is facilitated by market makers in various locations who interact through a computer network. The role of market makers is similar to that of specialists on trading floors: They indicate by computer their willingness to buy or sell shares of the stocks in which they make a market, and trades are executed through their interaction with other market makers.

For widely traded stocks, the spread between the bid and ask prices is very small, which is advantageous to investors. This means that if an investor who purchased shares changed his or her mind and immediately sold those shares, the loss would be minimal. However, when a stock is traded infrequently and its value is subject to much uncertainty, there is a wider spread between the bid price and the ask price. Under these conditions, an investor who purchases shares and then resells them in the market could incur a large loss. Consider a stock that has a bid price of $20 and an ask price of $20.40. There is a spread of $0.40 per share. In general, when you sell the stock, you will sell at the prevailing bid price. Thus, the bid price would have to increase by $.40 (or 2 percent) for you to just break even.

When you ask a broker to execute a trade, the broker decides on the route by which your order will be fulfilled. The spread quoted for a given stock may vary among market makers. Market makers sometimes compensate brokers for orders routed to them, so the market maker may use a wider spread in order to offer such a payment to the broker. An investor may pay only $8 to execute a buy order, but the order could be executed at a bid or ask price that reflects a wide spread.

Role of Electronic Communications Networks

Investors are increasingly relying on electronic communications networks (ECNs) to execute stock trades. For example, one type of ECN can accept buy limit orders and sell limit orders by organizing the orders by the price at which investors are willing to purchase a specific stock and matching up those orders with sell orders on the same stock. If the buy orders exceed the sell orders, it will accommodate only those buy orders that have a relatively high limit price.

The ECNs compete with specialists and market makers in the execution of orders. Consequently, the spreads between bid and ask quotes have become more narrow. Some investors engage in online trading, in which their online orders are transmitted by computer to an ECN. In these cases, the entire process from the time of the order until the fulfillment of the order is handled by computers.

BUYING STOCKS ON MARGIN

Investors who do not have sufficient funds to buy the stocks that they wish to buy can borrow a portion of their funds from their broker. The process of the investor's using some of her or his own funds along with some borrowed funds is referred to as buying the stock on margin. Funds are bor-rowed from the brokerage firm, and interest is paid on the borrowed funds. At least 50 percent of the funds an investor uses for a transaction must be provided in cash by the investor. Buying on margin is not recommended because it can be very risky, for reasons that will be illustrated shortly.

Investors must establish a margin account with their broker, in which they pledge some cash as collateral. This initial deposit is referred to as the *initial margin*. The broker will also specify a *maintenance margin,* or the minimum percentage of the stock's value that the investor must maintain. When a stock's value declines, investors who buy on margin may receive a margin call from their broker, in which they are asked to provide additional collateral. If investors do not have additional cash that they can pledge, they may be forced to sell the stock at that time. Investors who do not have additional collateral available should not even consider buying on margin. Even those investors who have adequate col-lateral should not buy stocks on margin unless they fully understand the risk that can result from financial leverage (as explained next) and want to take that risk.

Return from Buying on Margin

The return on a stock purchased on margin is affected by the proportion of the investment that is made with borrowed funds. Over short-term periods, the return (R) on stocks purchased on margin can be estimated as follows:

$$R = (\text{SP} - \text{invest} - \text{repay} + \text{div})/\text{invest}$$

where SP = selling price
invest = amount of the investment made with your own funds
repay = amount of loan repayment
div = dividend payment

For example, suppose that you can purchase 100 shares of stock for $80 per share. The total purchase price is $8000. You have $4000 in cash, and you borrow the remaining $4000 at an interest rate of 12 percent per year (1 percent per month). After 1 month, you sell your stock for $88 per share (or a total of $8800) and pay off your loan. Your loan repayment is $4040, which includes 1 percent interest on the amount that you borrowed. The return on the stock is what you have above and beyond your initial investment after paying off the loan.

In this example, your return is

$$R = (\$8800 - \$4000 - \$4040)/\$4000$$
$$= 19\%$$

If you had not borrowed funds when you invested in the stock, your return would have been

$$R = (\$8800 - \$8000)/\$8000$$
$$= 10\%$$

In this case, buying on margin would have almost doubled the return on your investment.

The disadvantage of buying on margin is that it will also magnify losses. For example, if the stock price was \$72 when you sold it after 1 month, your return from buying this stock on margin would be

$$R = (\$7200 - \$4000 - \$4040)/\$4000$$
$$= -21\%$$

If you had not borrowed funds when you invested in the stock, your return would have been

$$R = (\$7200 - \$8000)/\$8000$$
$$= -10\%$$

Thus, in this example, the loss you incurred when you bought on margin is more than twice the loss you would have incurred if you had not borrowed funds.

These examples show that buying on margin both increases potential return and increases your risk. Some investors do not recognize the risk. Others understand the risk, but reject the possibility that a stock's price may decline. History has shown that stocks can decline abruptly, and investors should consider that possibility before buying stocks on margin. Some investors may rationalize their investment by thinking that if the stock price declines, they will simply hold the stock until the price recovers and generates a gain for them. There are many cases in which the stock price never recovers, but instead moves toward zero. In this case, investors not only lose their initial investment but still need to repay the broker for the loan. There are also some cases in which investors are required to deposit more funds with the brokerage firm if the market value of their existing position declines. If the investors can not provide the additional funds required, the brokerage firm may close out the investor's position.

SHORT SELLING

When investors sense that a stock's performance will weaken in the future, they can capitalize on this by selling the stock short. This means that they borrow stock and sell it. At a future point in time, they plan to purchase the stock and return it to the investor from whom they borrowed it. If the stock has declined between the time they sold it and the time they purchase it, they can benefit.

Suppose that Stock Y is priced at $40 per share. It does not pay a dividend. You believe that Stock Y's price will decline in the near future. You contact your broker and ask to sell 100 shares of that stock short. Your broker essentially borrows this stock from another investor and sells it for you. You receive $4000 from the sale of the stock. As time passes, the stock price begins to decline. When it reaches $34, you contact your broker and request the purchase of 100 shares of Stock Y. The broker returns these shares to the investor from whom he or she borrowed them. You gained $6 per share, or $600, from your short position. When a stock pays dividends, you will need to pay dividends to the investor from whom the stock was borrowed while the short position is in effect.

Some investors use short sales to take advantage of a firm's weak management. For example, if a firm has used faulty accounting methods to inflate its earnings, an investor who recognizes that the earnings are compromised may consider shorting the stock. However, there is substantial risk to selling a stock short. Even if the investor has correctly guessed that the earnings are contrived, it is difficult to determine when the market will recognize that the stock's valuation is excessive. Consider the case of Enron. If someone had recognized in 1997 that Enron's earnings were inflated, and had taken a short position, the value of that position would have weakened over the next few years as the stock price rose. The market did not recognize that Enron's value was overestimated until 2002.

Given the potential risk, short sales are not recommended for the conservative investor. An unexpected increase in the stock can cause major losses to investors who take short positions.

B

THE DANGER OF INITIAL PUBLIC OFFERINGS

I n recent years, much media attention has been directed toward initial public offerings (IPOs) because of the potentially large returns that they may generate. An IPO is a first-time offering of stock to the public by a specific firm. Firms tend to consider IPOs when they are growing and are near their debt capacity, yet need additional funds to achieve their business plans. Some investors have earned very high returns by investing in a stock at the time of the IPO. However, many investors have lost their entire investment by investing in IPOs.

When you are considering an investment in an IPO, assess the details behind the IPO. What will the firm do with the funds obtained from the IPO? Are the firm's expansion plans rational? Is the price of the IPO reasonable? When the founders of a firm decide to do an IPO, they are essentially giving other investors a stake in their firm's profitability. The proportion of the firm owned by the founders is reduced after the IPO. Thus, founders should be willing to do an IPO only if the new shares can be sold at a high enough price to generate substantial new funds for the firm. In other words, the founders are not just giving their firm away. And if the firm can sell shares at a high price, some founders may even decide to cash out by selling their shares.

FINANCIAL DISCLOSURE BEFORE THE IPO

When firms engage in an IPO, they must disclose detailed financial information to prospective investors. They hire a securities firm that acts as a lead underwriter, placing the shares of stock with investors. Before placing the shares, the underwriter helps the issuing firm to develop its prospectus and price the offering. The prospectus summarizes the issuing firm's business plan and provides financial statements indicating its recent performance. The prospectus is filed with the Securities and Exchange Commission (SEC), which attempts to ensure that all relevant information is disclosed to investors.

The SEC focuses on whether facts are properly stated, rather than on whether the business plan makes sense. Investors are responsible for determining whether the business plan is viable. In the late 1990s, the business plans of many Internet firms lacked substance. However, the market sentiment was so favorable that many investors simply ignored the business plans and were willing to invest in any new Internet firm.

In 2001, the speculative bubble burst, and Internet stock prices plummeted. Investors learned a costly lesson, and they now tend to require that firms have a valid business plan before investing in IPOs. Investors are also paying more attention to the firm's performance before going public. However, the very flexible accounting guidelines give firms the opportunity to make their performance look better. Investors should question whether the issuing firm is overstating its condition and its potential in order to ensure that it will be able to attract a strong demand for its shares at the IPO.

TIMING THE IPO

There is some evidence that a firm's operating performance tends to peak at the time of its IPO, which suggests that firms use accounting flexibility to their advantage. While it is understandable that firms market themselves in order to raise funds, investors must cut through the hype to determine which firms have real substance. For those firms that have substance, investors must also determine whether their value per share exceeds the price at which the shares are being sold at the IPO. Some firms are able to inflate their earnings just before the IPO so that they are able to sell their shares at a high price.

THE SELLING PROCESS

After the prospectus has been approved by the SEC, it is sent to institutional investors who may want to purchase large blocks of stock in the IPO. The issuing firm and the lead underwriter may do a road show, in which they travel to cities in which there are many institutional investors and present the business plan.

During the road show, the lead underwriter gauges the level of demand for the shares at different possible offer prices. The offer price should ensure sufficient demand for all the shares to be sold. However, the underwriter wants to sell the shares at a high enough price for the offering to generate a sufficient amount of funds for the issuing firm. The price that investors are willing to pay is partially influenced by the existing market conditions. When the market is performing well, it is easier to place new shares with investors at a high price. The price is also dependent on the issuing firm's past performance and its potential. In general, the offer price is usually set at a level at which there is more demand for the shares than the supply of shares for sale. Consequently, the underwriter allocates the shares to its most favored institutional investors.

The lead underwriter organizes a syndicate (group) of securities firms that will help it place the shares with institutional investors. On the morning of the IPO, the syndicate sells the shares to those institutional investors that previously indicated an interest in buying shares.

RETURNS FROM INVESTING IN IPOs

The initial return (over the first day) on IPOs has averaged 20 percent over the last 30 years, and this is the main reason that many investors are intrigued by IPOs. In fact, in the 1998–1999 period, the return on many Internet stocks exceeded 70 percent.

Some institutional investors recognize the tendency for IPOs to produce high initial returns, followed by a downward drift in price. They capitalize on this tendency by "flipping" their shares, which involves investing in IPOs and then selling their shares in the secondary market a few hours or days later. This action can cause the stock price to decline shortly after the IPO.

The investors who receive the unusually high initial returns at the time of the IPO are those who are able to purchase the stock at the offer price. By the time individual investors are able to purchase shares, the stock price is already much higher than the offer price.

Returns to Individual Investors

There are some well-known cases in which individual investors have earned very large returns from investing in IPOs. However, the risk of IPOs is well documented. Many individuals have lost their entire investment when they invested in IPOs. If the IPO is fully subscribed, the entire issue is placed with the institutional investors. Later in the day of the IPO or in the following day, some institutional investors may sell some of the shares that they purchased at a much higher price if there is sufficient demand. For example, the offer price set on the morning of the IPO may be $20 per share. If the issue is fully subscribed, the only way that an individual investor will be able to buy shares is if an institutional investor who invested in the IPO is willing to sell those shares in the secondary market. The price of the shares of stock in the secondary market is not the offer price, but whatever price the market will bear. If the demand for shares is strong, the secondary market price of the stock may be $30, and the institutional investor's return is 50 percent in one day. The return for the individual investor will depend on the price at which she or he sells the shares in the future. In general, stock prices of IPOs tend to drift downward over time after the first day or so. Consequently, those individual investors who invest in an IPO stock at the end of the first day tend to earn poor returns.

EFFECT OF LOCKUP RESTRICTIONS

Once the stock is listed on a stock exchange, investors who hold shares can sell them on that exchange, while other investors who want to invest in the stock can buy them on the exchange. At this point, the founders of a firm have the opportunity to sell their shares. The underwriter attempts to prevent the founders from selling their shares shortly after the IPO in order to ensure stability in the stock price. These lockup restrictions usually expire in 6 months. Once the lockup restriction is removed, there may be even more downward pressure on the stock price, because the founders can sell their shares in the secondary market. There is clear evidence that the stock prices of IPO firms typically decline at the time the lockup restriction expires.

CONCERNS ABOUT THE IPO PROCESS

The IPO process is presently being assessed for possible unethical behavior. Some underwriters provide the CEOs of firms that might go public in the near future with shares of other IPOs. The shares are sold to these CEOs at the offer price. The return on shares that can be purchased at the offer price is usually high. It can be argued that this special deal provided by investment banks to CEOs is a payoff in anticipation of the CEO's steering future business to the investment bank. For example, suppose that an investment bank (IB) is about to serve as underwriter for a firm (Firm X) that is going public. IB knows that Firm Y and Firm Z also plan to go public in the near future. IB is competing with other investment banks to serve as the underwriter of the future IPOs by Firm Y and Firm Z. IB informs the CEOs of Firm Y and Firm Z that it is willing to sell them shares from the IPO of Firm X at the offer price. The CEOs of Firm Y and Firm Z will probably earn large returns on their investment because IB allowed them to purchase shares at the offer price. IB expects that the CEOs of these two firms will return the favor by steering future business to IB. That is, these CEOs may suggest to their respective boards of directors that their firm hire IB as the underwriter for their own firm's IPO, or for other business. The typical fee charged for serving as underwriter in an IPO is 7 percent of the offering. Since most offerings exceed $40 million, the underwriting fee is usually at least $3 million.

When firms engage in an IPO, the investment bank that served as lead underwriter tends to have one of its analysts assign a rating to the firm. In virtually all cases, the analyst from the investment bank that also served as underwriter assigns the highest rating possible to the firm over the next several months. It is commonly argued that the investment banks use the analyst's high rating to prevent the firm's stock price from declining. Thus, the firm that engaged in an IPO benefits from a price that is somewhat inflated or stabilized after the IPO. The investment bank that underwrites the IPO benefits in the form of fees charged to the firm. The only potential loser is the individual investor who was not able to obtain shares at the offer price, who will likely pay too much for the shares she or he purchased.

One might argue that the IPO shares sold at the offer price to CEOs of other firms are a cost of obtaining new business. However, some CEOs have made millions of dollars from holding these shares for just a short period. This suggests that the shares could have been sold at a higher offer price, which would have generated more funds for the firm whose shares were being sold during the IPO.

Index

About the Author

Jeff Madura is the SunTrust Bank Professor of Finance at Florida Atlantic University. Professor Madura is the author of numerous journal publications related to stock valuation, and is also the author of several popular financial textbooks, including *International Financial Management*, and *Financial Markets and Institutions*.